Business Auto

COMMERCIAL LINES COVERAGE GUIDE

David D. Thamann,
J.D., CPCU, ARM

The
National
Underwriter
Company
A Unit of Highline Media LLC

> This publication is designed to provide accurate and authoritative information in regard to the subject matter covered. It is sold with the understanding that the publisher is not engaged in rendering legal, accounting, or other professional service. If legal advice or other expert assistance is required, the services of a competent professional person should be sought. — from a Declaration of Principles jointly adopted by a Committee of the American Bar Association and a Committee of Publishers and Associations.

Copyright © 2004, 1998 by
THE NATIONAL UNDERWRITER COMPANY
P.O. Box 14367
Cincinnati, Ohio 45250-0367

Second Printing

All rights reserved. No part of this book may be reproduced in any form or by any means without permission in writing from the publisher.

Includes copyrighted material of Insurance Services Office, Inc., with its permission.

This product includes information which is proprietary to Insurance Services Office, Inc. ISO does not guarantee the accuracy or timeliness of the ISO information provided. ISO shall not be liable for any loss or damage of any kind and howsoever caused resulting from your use of the ISO information.

International Standard Book Number: 0-87218-716-0

Printed in the United States of America

Table of Contents

Chapter 1: The Business Auto Coverage Form, 1
    ISO Rules, 1
    The Declarations Form, 2
    Purpose of this Work, 3

Chapter 2: Covered Auto Designations,
    Coverage Symbols, 5
        Symbol 1, 5
        Symbol 2, 6
        Symbol 3, 6
        Symbol 4, 7
        Symbol 5, 7
        Symbol 6, 7
        Symbol 7, 8
        Symbol 8, 8
        Symbol 9, 9
    Owned Autos Acquired After Policy Inception, 11
    Certain Trailers, Mobile Equipment, and
        Temporary Substitute Autos, 12

Chapter 3: Liability Coverage, 15

    The Insuring Agreement, 15
    Who Is An Insured, 18
    Coverage Extensions, 19
    Exclusions, 20
        Expected or Intended Injury, 20
        Contractual, 21
        Workers Compensation/Employers Liability, 21
        Care, Custody, or Control, 23
        Handling of Property, 24
        Movement of Property, 25
        Operation of Mobile Equipment, 25
        Completed Operations, 26
        Pollution, 26

       War, 28
       Racing, 28
  Limits of Insurance, 29

Chapter 4: Physical Damage Coverage, 31
  The Coverage Agreements, 31
       Towing, 33
       Glass Breakage, 34
  Coverage Extension, 35
  Exclusions (Physical Damage), 36
  Limits of Insurance, 39
  Deductibles, 41

Chapter 5: Business Auto Conditions, 43
  Loss Conditions, 43
       Appraisal, 43
       Duties in the Event of Loss, 44
       Legal Action Against the Insurer, 45
       Loss Payment, 45
       Transfer of the Rights of Recovery, 46
  General Conditions, 47
       Bankruptcy, 47
       Concealment, Misrepresentation, or Fraud, 47
       Liberalization, 48
       No Benefit to Bailee, 48
       Other Insurance, 49
       Premium Audit, 49
       Policy Period/Coverage Territory, 50
       Two or More Coverage Forms, 51
  Common Policy Conditions, 51
       Cancellation, 52
       Changes, 52
       Examination of Books, 52
       Inspections and Surveys, 53
       Premiums, 53
       Transfer of rights and Duties, 53

Chapter 6: Business Auto Definitions, 55
  "Accident", 55
  "Auto", 55
  "Bodily Injury", 56
  "Covered Pollution Cost or Expense", 57

"Diminution in Value", 58
"Employee", 58
"Insured", 58
"Insured Contract", 59
"Leased Worker", 61
"Loss", 61
"Mobile Equipment", 62
"Pollutants", 63
"Property Damage", 63
"Suit", 63
"Temporary Worker", 63
"Trailer", 65

Chapter 7: Auto Medical Payments Coverage, 67
Coverage, 67
Who Is An Insured, 69
Exclusions, 70
Limit of Insurance, 73
Changes in Conditions, 74
Additional Definitions, 74

Chapter 8: Nonownership Coverage, 77
Hired or Borrowed Autos Coverage, 78
Hired Autos Rating Information, 81
Nonownership Liability Insurance, 81
Who Is An Insured, 83
Nonownership Property Damage Coverage, 84
Rating Information, 84

Chapter 9: Auto Leasing & Rental Coverage Endorsements, 87
Lessor—Additional Insured and Loss Payee, 87
Contingent Coverage CA 20 09, 88
Conversion, Embezzlement or
  Secretion Coverage CA 20 10, 89
Exclusion of Certain Leased Autos CA 20 11, 91
Rent-It-Here/Leave-It-Here Autos CA 20 12, 91
Schedule of Limits for Owned Autos CA 20 13, 92
Second Level Coverage CA 20 14, 93
Autos Leased with Drivers CA 20 33, 93
Conclusion, 94

Chapter 10: Drive Other Car Coverage Endorsements, 95
    Broadened Coverage for Named Individuals CA 99 10, 96
    Individual Named Insured CA 99 17, 98

Chapter 11: Endorsements, 101
    Mobile Equipment Subject to
        Motor Vehicle Insurance Laws CA 00 51, 101
    Limited Mexico Coverage CA 01 21, 102
    Sound Receiving Equipment Coverage —
        Fire, Police and Emergency Vehicles CA 20 02, 103
    Drive-Away Contractors CA 20 05, 104
    Driving Schools CA 20 06, 104
    Mobile Equipment CA 20 15, 105
    Mobile Homes Contents Coverage CA 20 16, 105
    Professional Services Not Covered, CA 20 18, 107
    Repossessed Autos CA 20 19, 107
    Snowmobiles CA 20 21, 108
    Registration Plates Not Issued for a Specific Auto CA 20 27, 108
    Autos Leased, Hired, Rented or Borrowed With Drivers —
        Physical Damage Coverage CA 20 33, 109
    Designated Insured CA 20 48, 109
    Explosives CA 23 01, 109
    Multi-Purpose Equipment CA 23 03, 110
    Rolling Stores CA 23 04, 110
    Wrong Delivery of Liquid Products CA 23 05, 110
    Coverage for Injury to Leased Workers CA 23 25, 111
    Public Transportation Autos CA 24 02, 111
    Fire; Fire and Theft; Theft and Windstorm;
     and Limited Specified Causes of Loss Coverages CA 99 14, 112
    Rental Reimbursement Coverage CA 99 23, 112
    Stated Amount Insurance CA 99 28, 113
    Tapes, Records, and Discs Coverage CA 99 30, 113
    Employees As Insureds CA 99 33, 114
    Social Service Agencies—
        Volunteers As Insureds CA 99 34, 114
    Garagekeepers Coverage CA 99 37, 114
    Exclusion or Excess Coverage Hazards
        Otherwise Insured CA 99 40, 115
    Loss Payable Clause CA 99 44, 115
    Employee As Lessor CA 99 47, 116
    Pollution Liability — Broadened Covearge CA 99 48, 116
    Garagekeepers Coverage — Customers Sound

Receiving Equipment CA 99 59, 117
Audio, Visual and Data Electronic Equipment Coverage
       CA 99 60, 117
Loss Payable Clause — Audio, Visual and Data
       Electronic Equipment CA 99 61, 118
Uninsured Motorists Coverage Endorsements, 118

Appendixes, 119
  Appendix A: Commercial Auto Checklist, 119
  Appendix B: Table of Limits, 127
  Appendix C: Indicators of Vehicle Theft Fraud, 129
  Appendix D: Specimen Forms and Endorsements
         (Listed Numerically), 133
     CA 00 01 Business Auto Coverage Form, 135
     CA DS 03 Business Auto Declarations, 146
     CA 20 01 Additional Insured — Lessor, 152
     CA 99 03 Auto Medical Payments Coverage, 154
     CA 99 10 Drive Other Car Coverage —
       Broadened Coverage for Named Individuals, 156
     CA 99 16 Hired Autos Specified As Covered Autos You
       Own, 158
     CA 99 17 Individual Named Insured, 159
     CA 01 21 Limited Mexico Coverage, 161
     CA 20 48 Designated Insured, 162
     CA 20 54 Employee Hired Autos, 163
     CA 20 71 Auto Loan/Lease Gap Coverage, 164
     CA 00 51 Changes IN Coverage Forms, 165
     CA 20 15 Mobile Equipment, 166
     IL 00 17 Common Policy Conditions, 168

Index, 169

Coverage Scenarios

Application of the Wear & Tear Exclusion, 37

Does Borrowing Constitute Control? 9

Employee-Caused Damage Within Insured's Care, Custody or Control? 23

Is Loss of Use A Covered Loss? 61

Is The Vehicle Considered Mobile Equipment or An Auto? 56

Labor Costs, 34

"Permissive Use" of Named Insured's Auto, 10

"Reasonable Belief" For Auto Use, 72

Separation of Insureds, 59

Is Symbol 8 The Proper Symbol for (Hired Auto Liability) Coverage? 80

What Are The "Expenses Incurred?" 68

What Is A Private Passenger Auto? 6

What Is Collision? 32

When Is Electronic Equipment Permanently Installed? 38

When Does Duty to Defend End? 17

When Must Services Be Rendered To Be Covered Under Med Pay? 69

Which Policy Covers – CGL or BAP? 24

Acknowledgement

The author wants to express his appreciation to Karen Combs, Assistant to the Editor, and the staff of National Underwriter's Editorial Composition Department, Georgia Barry, Manager, for the expeditious handling of this book.

D.T.

1

The Business Auto Coverage Form

The Insurance Services Office (ISO) files on behalf of its member companies four standardized policies for insuring commercial automobiles: the business auto coverage form, the truckers coverage form, the garage coverage form, and the motor carrier coverage form. All of these coverage forms are worthy of an in-depth discussion; however, the scope of this book is limited to the 10/01 edition of the business auto policy (or the BAP), CA 00 01.

CA 00 01 is the most widely used policy in the commercial auto program of ISO. Like other ISO coverage forms, the BAP is combined with a declarations form, common policy conditions, and any applicable endorsements to be used as either a monoline policy or as one coverage part in a multi-line, or package, policy. Private passenger type autos, as well as other types of autos, owned by corporations, partnerships, unincorporated associations, individuals, or government agencies can be insured under CA 00 01. Nonowned and hired autos can also be insured under the BAP.

ISO Rules

The general rules governing the writing of coverage under the business auto coverage form are found in Division One of the Commercial Lines Manual (CLM). A review of some of the basic rules is helpful in discussing and analyzing CA 00 01.

Policies may be written for a specific term of one, two, or three years, or on a continuous basis. A policy may be renewed by renewal certificates which must conform in every respect to current rules, rates, and forms at the time of renewal. Premiums for the policies, whether new or renewal, are computed at the rates in effect at the time of the policy inception or policy renewal.

In addition to the conditions found on the business auto coverage form itself, common policy conditions form IL 00 17 is also used with the BAP. IL 00 17 contains six conditions that apply to the BAP: cancellation, changes, examination of the named insured's books and records, inspections and surveys, premiums, and transfer of rights and duties.

If a resident agent's countersignature is required by state law, the Resident Agent Countersignature endorsement, IL 09 17, is attached to the BAP; this is the rule, unless state law prohibits the use of the endorsement or so restricts the use as to make it inappropriate.

More than one interest may be named on the policy and rated as a single risk if one interest owns more than 50% of another. All the interests that are combined must be named on the policy.

Other rules applicable to the BAP may be noted throughout this book and are placed in relation to the coverage(s) being discussed.

The Declarations Form

The business auto declarations form, CA DS 03, is attached to the auto coverage form in order to publicize basic information about the insured, the type of coverage bought by the insured, endorsements attached to the BAP that modify coverage granted under CA 00 01, and premiums paid for the exposures insured.

Item one of the dec form lists the named insured, mailing address, and policy period. The type of business is also specified—corporation, partnership, limited liability company, individual, or other; this is relevant to the discussion of who is an insured under the BAP.

Item two of the dec form is a schedule of coverages and covered autos. The policy provides only those coverages where an amount is shown in the premium column of item two. For example, if the insured wants liability coverage for his or her auto, a premium charge has to be shown on the dec form for that coverage; this also applies to physical damage coverage, medical payments, or any other relevant coverage. Item two also has a column for the insured to show a symbol for the covered autos. There are nine symbols to describe covered autos under CA 00 01, ranging from symbol 1 to symbol 9 (these symbols will be discussed more fully in Chapter 2). For example, if the insured wants liability coverage for any auto, he or she puts the symbol "1" in the column next to the liability coverage; if the insured wants collision coverage for specifically described autos only, he or she puts the symbol "7" in the column next to the physical damage—collision coverage. Because coverage under CA 00 01 is for "covered autos," the insured must enter the proper symbol on the declarations form to make sure that the proper auto is given the desired coverage.

Item three is a schedule of covered autos that the named insured owns. This schedule asks the insured to describe the covered owned auto(s), list the cost of the auto(s), notes the city and state where the covered auto is principally garaged, and classify the covered auto as to its use (service, retail, commercial), age, and radius of operation. The classification information aids the insurer in the rating process for the covered autos. This item also offers a summary of the premiums, limits, and deductibles for the owned covered autos, on an auto by auto, coverage by coverage basis.

Item four is a schedule of hired or borrowed covered auto coverage and premiums. The schedule shows if the insured has liability and physical damage coverages for hired or borrowed autos, the estimated cost of the hire, the rate per each $100 cost of hire, and the premium for the coverages.

Item five is the schedule for nonownership liability coverage. The number of employees, partners, or volunteers (for social service agency insureds) is noted in item five for rating purposes.

Item six is the schedule for gross receipts or mileage used for rating purposes for liability coverage for public auto or leasing rental concerns. If the insured is in the business of transporting passengers, mail, or merchandise and uses CA 00 01 for insurance coverages, the gross receipts and mileage listed in item six offer the rating bases for the charged premium. The same is true if the insured rents or leases autos to others.

Purpose of This Work

The purpose of this book is to review the business auto coverage form and issues arising out of its use. Examples making coverage or claims settlements points are used throughout the chapters of the book, as are coverage scenarios adapted from correspondence between the editorial staff of National Underwriter's FC&S and its subscribers.

This work joins a number of books published by the National Underwriter Company reviewing and analyzing individual insurance forms. Among these are *Commercial General Liability*, the *Businessowners Policy Coverage Guide*, the *Commercial Property Coverage Guide*, the *Personal Auto Coverage Guide*, the *Homeowners Coverage Guide*, and the *Business Interruption Book*.

2

Covered Auto Designations

Coverage Symbols

The business auto coverage form, CA 00 01, uses nine symbols to describe covered autos. These coverage symbols are used in item two of the declarations to signal which autos qualify as covered autos for each coverage being purchased by the insured. Unless there is a coverage symbol shown beside the coverage name, the coverage will not apply. And, unless the correct coverage symbol is shown, the insured may be without coverage that it intended to have. The symbols are numerals ranging from "1" through "9."

Symbol 1

Symbol 1 signifies "any auto." The use of symbol 1 makes any auto a covered auto. The insured will have coverage for any auto owned, hired, borrowed, or used by the insured. When symbol 1 is used, there is no need to indicate any other coverage symbol because symbol 1 encompasses all of them. Any auto that the insured acquires during the policy period is automatically covered and need not be reported to the insurance company before the insurer conducts an audit of exposures (which ordinarily occurs at the end of the policy period).

From the insured's perspective, symbol 1 is clearly the best choice for coverage. Of course, since the coverage is so broad, the premium charged is appropriately high. The insured has to decide if the peace of mind of having its auto exposures so broadly covered is equal to the price paid.

Symbol 2

Symbol 2 is for "owned autos only". The named insured uses this symbol if he or she wants coverage only for autos that are owned; this symbol is not to be used for hired, borrowed, and nonowned autos. Symbol 2 provides automatic coverage for any auto that the named insured acquires ownership of during the policy period. Also, if symbol 2 is used for liability coverage, it extends that coverage to cover trailers or semitrailers that the named insured does not own while they are attached to power units that the named insured does own. Again, symbol 2 can be used to extend the coverages offered by the BAP to any owned auto.

Symbol 3

Symbol 3 is for "owned private passenger autos only." This classification includes private passenger autos that the named insured acquires ownership of during the policy period.

The coverage umbrella for this symbol is slightly smaller than when symbol 2 is used; the auto must be a private passenger auto and not just any owned auto. However, the BAP does not define a "private passenger auto" so this can lead to disputes over just what that term includes.

What is a Private Passenger Auto?

An insured corporation has a business auto policy using symbol 3—owned private passenger autos only—for the liability and physical damage coverages. The insured bought a motor home for the use of its officers and employees for events like tailgating at football games. At one of these events, the motor home was damaged by a collision with a concrete wall. The insurer declined coverage, stating that the motor home was not a private passenger auto. The insured believes the loss is covered since the term "private passenger auto" is not defined on the policy.

The insured is usually entitled to have the policy interpreted in its favor if there is any ambiguity in the wording. And, since the term "private passenger auto" is not defined on the policy, the insured might have a sympathetic judge grant coverage. However, two things work against such an interpretation: the definition of private passenger auto found in the commercial lines manual (CLM) and common sense.

The CLM defines a private passenger auto as a four-wheel auto of the private passenger or station wagon type, including a pickup, panel truck, or van that is not used for business. The implication is clear that something as big and heavy as a motor home is not considered a private passenger auto by the insurer. Also, when most people refer

(scenario continues next page)

> *(continued from previous page)*
>
> to private passenger cars, they normally don't include motor homes in that category; common sense calls for separating the two. This is not to say that the BAP is not meant to apply to a motor home, but that symbols 1 (any auto), 2 (owned autos only), 4 (owned autos other than private passenger autos), or 7 (specifically described autos) are more appropriate for such coverage. By using those symbols, both the insured and the insurer will recognize the proper exposures and be able to develop a fair and adequate premium.

Symbol 4

Symbol 4 refers to "owned autos other than private passenger autos only;" this includes autos of the same type that the named insured acquires ownership of during the policy period. When used for liability coverage, symbol 4 also includes nonowned trailers or semitrailers while attached to power units owned by the named insured. When seen in contrast to symbol 3, symbol 4 provides evidence that the insurer sees a distinction between private passenger type autos and other than private passenger types.

Symbol 5

Symbol 5 designates "owned autos subject to no-fault." This symbol is for autos owned by the named insured that are required by law to have no-fault coverage in the state where the autos are licensed or principally garaged. Autos that the named insured acquires ownership of during the policy period are automatically covered if they are also required to have no-fault benefits. Symbol 5 is not appropriate in states where the named insured has the right to buy no-fault coverages, *but is not required to do so by law*. If the insured does choose to purchase no-fault coverage in one of these states, the symbol used by the insured to describe the covered autos is not crucial to the no-fault endorsement's coverage; a symbol (any one except symbol 5) would still have to be chosen for the coverages afforded under the BAP, of course, but that would not affect coverage under the no-fault endorsement.

Symbol 6

Symbol 6 is for "owned autos subject to a compulsory uninsured motorists law." This symbol applies to autos owned by the named insured that, because of the law in the state where the autos are licensed or principally garaged, must have uninsured motorists (UM) coverage; the insured can not reject the coverage. Symbol 6 does include autos that the named insured acquires ownership of during the policy period. Symbol 6 is not appropriate in states where the named insured has the right to buy UM coverage, but is not required to do so by law.

Symbol 7

Symbol 7 is for "specifically described autos." If symbol 7 is used, only those autos described in item three of the declarations form, for which a premium is charged, are covered. Symbol 7 does include, for liability coverage, any trailers not owned by the named insured while attached to any power unit described in item three. Recall that item three on the declarations form is a highly descriptive list of autos owned by the named insured; the year, model, make, body type, VIN (vehicle identification number), cost, and classification of covered autos are all supposed to be written in item three. It should not surprise anyone, then, that if an auto owned by the named insured is not listed in item three, and symbol 7 is used, that unlisted auto will not be considered a covered auto by the insurer.

Symbol 8

Symbol 8 signifies "hired autos only." These are autos that the named insured leases, hires, rents, or borrows. Not included are autos leased, hired, rented, or borrowed from any of the named insured's employees, partners, members (of a limited liability company), or members of their households. When symbol 8 is used for liability or physical damage coverage, the hired auto coverage schedule in item four of the declarations must be completed. This schedule shows the estimated cost incurred by the insured for hiring autos, the rate per $100 cost of hire, and the resultant premium charged for the coverage bought by the insured. Of course, this premium is only for those autos that are known to be leased, hired, rented, or borrowed at the inception date of the policy. If the named insured hires or rents a car during the policy period, that car is automatically a covered auto under symbol 8 and the insurer will pick up any additional premium at the premium audit at policy's end.

Remember that a hired auto is not owned by the named insured and that the BAP declares that the insurance provided for autos not owned by the named insured is excess over any other collectible insurance. The key word here is "collectible;" if there is other insurance on the hired auto that can not be collected for whatever reason, the named insured's BAP will revert to primary coverage. Also, when it comes to hired auto physical damage coverage, any covered auto leased, hired, rented, or borrowed by the named insured is deemed to be an auto owned by the named insured and thus, on a primary insurance basis under the named insured's BAP.

If an auto is leased, hired, or rented, that status is usually made clear through the use of a contract which identifies the auto(s) as leased, hired, or rented. Should a loss to the auto(s) occur, the use of symbol 8 on the BAP allows coverage to apply to the identified auto(s). However, a problem could arise over the term "borrowed," that is, just when is a car borrowed? Remember, the term "borrowed" is not defined in the business auto policy.

> **Does Borrowing Constitute Control?**
>
> *A person used his car to pick up something for the ABC Company which had a business auto policy using symbol 8 for coverage purposes. After a loss occurred, the insurer denied coverage for the named insured, declaring that ABC did not actually possess or control the car and so, could not have "borrowed" the car. The insured felt that since ABC was receiving a benefit from the car's use, that in effect meant the insured borrowed the car.*
>
> The insurer is on solid ground in denying the claim. The majority legal view is that the term "borrow" connotes much more than merely receiving some benefit from the use of another's vehicle. "Borrowing" a car requires taking possession of something; that is, there must be some element of substantial control or dominion over the vehicle in order for it to be considered "borrowed." Besides, the insured chose a symbol of coverage (symbol 8) that described only those autos leased, hired, rented, or borrowed. The auto policy has other symbols that would have given the insured coverage in a situation such as this—either symbol 1, any auto, or symbol 9, which includes nonowned autos used in connection with the named insured's business.

Symbol 9

Symbol 9 is used for "nonowned autos only." This category is for those autos that the named insured does not own, lease, hire, rent, or borrow that are used in connection with the named insured's business. It also includes autos owned by the named insured's employees, partners, members (of a limited liability company), or members of their households; but this is only while the autos are used in the named insured's business or personal affairs. And, even though the description of symbol 9 does not mention it, the symbol also includes the car of anyone (other than the named insured) used in connection with the named insured's business; so, if a friend of the named insured uses his or her own car to run an errand for the named insured, that auto is considered a covered auto if symbol 9 is on the insured's auto policy.

Note that symbol 9 refers to autos that the named insured does not own, lease, hire, rent, or borrow. This ambiguity could lead to some coverage questions.

> ### "Permissive Use" of Named Insured's Auto
>
> *The named insured under a business auto policy is The ABC Corporation. Symbol 9 is used to designate its covered autos. The president of ABC has his own private passenger auto insured under a personal auto policy. The president asked a neighbor to use his (the president's) auto to deliver a package of documents concerning the corporation's business to an accountant's office. The neighbor was involved in an at-fault accident and the injured party sued ABC Corp. The insurer denied any coverage since the president of ABC owned the car and the BAP specified nonowned coverage only. The president is arguing for coverage as the auto was not owned by the named insured.*
>
> *The insured is correct in his viewpoint. The named insured on the BAP is ABC Corporation, not the president of the company. Symbol 9 is for autos not owned by the named insured, and even if the president of the named insured company owns an auto in his name, this does not translate into an auto owned by the named insured under the BAP.*

If the named insured has chosen nonownership liability coverage, item five on the declarations must be completed. This schedule lists the rating basis and premium for the liability coverage. For rating purposes, insureds are divided into two categories: social service agencies or other than social service agencies.

Obviously, most insureds are other than social service agencies; but, for clarification purposes, a social service agency auto is defined as "an auto used by a governmental entity, civic, charitable, or social service organization to provide transportation to clients incident to the social services sponsored by the organization." An example of this would be an employee of United Appeal using his own car to drive clients to a store or medical facility. The separate rating process for social service agencies simply recognizes the increased risks that this example entails. As for the "other than social service agencies," the liability rating basis uses the number of employees or partners to develop a premium. However, these categories fail to take into consideration the members of a limited liability company. A limited liability company is essentially a cross between a partnership and a corporation whose participants are called "members," not employees or partners. Presumably, to ease any rating problems, the insurer could simply call the members of a limited liability company "employees" of the named insured, but the insured and the insurer should clarify this point prior to policy inception.

Owned Autos Acquired After Policy Inception

This section of CA 00 01 deals with autos that the named insured acquires during the policy period. The two key words in this provision are: "owned" and "acquired."

This provision is for autos that are described using Symbols 1 through 7. Symbols 2 through 6 specifically describe owned autos. Symbol 1, being extremely broad, applies to both owned and nonowned autos. Symbol 7 does not directly address ownership of the autos, but it does encompass only those autos described in item three of the declarations form and that item is a schedule of "covered autos you own;" so, indirectly, the focus of Symbol 7 is on owned autos. No doubt, the insured can use hired autos and nonowned autos during the policy period and have coverage under the BAP (through Symbols 8 and 9 respectively), but the insurer details in this section what type of coverage exists for owned autos acquired during the policy period.

The other key word, "acquire," is somewhat open to interpretation as the BAP does not define it. Does it mean to simply take possession of or to acquire ownership of? If the insured buys an auto on Monday but does not take physical possession of it until Friday, has the insured acquired it for coverage purposes? If the insured buys an auto and takes possession of it, but the title has not yet been transferred, has the insured acquired that auto?

Since the auto policy does not define the word, the dictionary has to provide guidance. "Acquire" is defined by the tenth edition of *Merriam Webster's Collegiate Dictionary* as "to get as one's own, to come into possession or control of." Unfortunately, this does not clarify the matter very much. In such an instance, the insured has to be given the benefit of any doubt. If the insured obtains an auto by buying it, or if the insured obtains an auto by simply taking possession of it, the insured can make a valid case that he or she has acquired the auto. However, it would be wise for the insured, and a point in favor of coverage, if he or she notified the insurer immediately upon purchasing or acquiring another auto.

As for the coverage granted under this acquisition clause, that depends on the symbol(s) used by the insured at the policy inception.

If Symbols 1, 2, 3, 4, 5, or 6 are entered next to a coverage in item two of the declarations, the insured has the same coverage for the acquired autos for the remainder of the policy period. For example, if the insured has entered a covered auto designation symbol next to liability and physical damage collision coverages on the declarations, then the autos that the named insured acquires during the policy period have liability coverage and collision coverage automatically. If the insured has not entered a symbol next to, for example, medical payments coverage, then that coverage will not be afforded to any acquired autos. The insured will not automatically get any coverages for acquired autos that he did not purchase at or before the inception of the policy.

If Symbol 7 is entered next to a coverage in item two of the dec form, any auto that the named insured acquires will be a covered auto for that coverage only if two requirements are met: the insurer must already cover all autos that the named insured owns for that coverage, or the acquisition must replace an auto previously owned by the named insured that had that coverage; and, the named insured must tell the insurer within 30 days after the acquisition that that particular coverage is wanted. Therefore, if the insured has Symbol 7 next to liability coverage on the dec form, and then acquires another auto during the policy period, that same coverage will attach to the acquired auto, not automatically, but only if the stated conditions are met.

These two conditions both have to be fulfilled in order for "Symbol 7" coverage to attach for the remainder of the policy period. However, if the first condition is met, the insured does have coverage for at least 30 days even if he does not report to the insurer. After the 30 days have lapsed, the insured loses the coverage for the acquired auto if no notice has been given to the insurer.

Certain Trailers, Mobile Equipment and Temporary Substitute Autos

This section on covered auto designations deals with liability coverage. If liability coverage is provided under the BAP, the following types of vehicles are considered covered autos for liability coverage: certain trailers, mobile equipment under certain circumstances, and temporary substitutes.

The trailers must have a load capacity of 2,000 pounds (one ton) or less and be designed primarily for travel on public roads. Unfortunately, this description only serves to cloud the issue of coverage under the BAP. The definition of "auto" includes a trailer or semitrailer designed for travel on public roads. Therefore, if the insured has liability coverage using symbol 1— any auto—he should have liability coverage for any trailer. Is this coverage for any trailer now limited to trailers that have a load capacity of 2,000 pounds or less? Similarly, symbol 2 designates as a covered auto a nonowned trailer while attached to an owned power unit. Is the nonowned trailer a covered auto only if it has a load capacity of 2,000 pounds or less?

This clause is probably meant to serve as a limitation on trailer coverage, albeit a confusingly written one. The theory behind this limitation may be that the BAP should be used for smaller vehicles (such as private passenger type autos, vans, or pickup trucks) that can pull small trailers, that is trailers with a load capacity of 2,000 pounds or less. If the insured has larger vehicles and larger capacity trailers, the truckers coverage form and the motor carrier coverage form are available for those exposures.

Another possible purpose for this clause is rating. The 2,000 pound language may be simply a red flag to the insured and his agent that insurers want a limit on those trailers that are given automatic coverage. Trailers with a load capacity of 2,000 pounds or less can be insured automatically, but those over the 2,000 pound limit should be charged a premium.

A third possibility for the clause is that, in certain situations where the covered auto designation symbol does not include a trailer, the automatic trailer coverage can serve as a helpful tool for the insured. For example, designation symbol "3" is for owned private passenger autos only. If the insured chose symbol "3" for liability coverage and then bought a trailer or used a borrowed trailer for some reason, the covered auto symbol would not include that trailer (after all, a trailer is clearly not a private passenger auto). As another example, symbol "8" is for hired autos only. If the insured chose symbol "8" and then buys a trailer or perhaps borrows a trailer from an employee, then the chosen symbol would not properly provide coverage for the trailer. Another example is with symbol "9". This symbol is for nonowned autos only. If the insured has symbol "9" on his BAP and then buys a trailer or rents one in connection with his business, the trailer clause would provide liability coverage for the insured (as long as the load capacity is 2,000 pounds or less) to supplement the coverage provided by symbol "9".

In any case, in order to prevent a legal dispute over coverage for a trailer, the insurer should make it clear to the insured prior to the inception of the policy that trailers are covered autos under the BAP, with some possible limitations. The BAP will provide liability coverage for the exposure of using a trailer with a load capacity of 2,000 pounds or less, regardless of the designation symbol that the insured chose for his covered autos. If the insured uses a trailer with a heavier load capacity, the chosen covered auto designation symbol needs to be the proper one in order for the insured to receive the liability coverage he needs in his business.

In any case, the insured should list any known trailer exposures in the declarations prior to policy inception. This way, the parties to the insuring agreement are clear as to what is covered and the insured can seek coverage under another form if it has larger capacity trailers as a risk exposure.

Mobile equipment is usually not covered under an auto policy; the CGL form takes care of that. However, under CA 00 01, mobile equipment, while being carried or towed by a covered auto, is considered a covered auto for liability coverage. Note that the CGL form excludes BI or PD arising out of the transportation of mobile equipment by an auto owned or operated by an insured. This provision is meant to simplify coverage for the insured in case an accident occurs while a piece of mobile equipment is being towed by the insured with a covered auto.

For example, if the insured is using his covered auto to tow a forklift from one location to another, and an accident occurs on a public road wherein the forklift hits a car and injures the driver, the insured can seek coverage for any liability claim under the BAP. Even though the forklift is mobile equipment, there will be no dispute between the auto insurer and the general liability insurer as to which one will provide the coverage. The insured has the claim against him handled without any undue delays caused by insurers arguing over which one should cover the claim.

Finally, any auto that the named insured does not own, but is used with the permission of its owner as a temporary substitute for a covered auto the named insured owns that is out of service, is considered a covered auto under the named insured's BAP. The insured's own vehicle has to be out of service due to a breakdown, repair, servicing, loss, or destruction. The obvious example here is a "loaner" car; the insured takes his own auto in for repair and the garage loans one of its autos to the insured to use for the duration of the repair job. Note that, even though the loaner is a covered auto under the insured's BAP, the coverage is excess over the garage's insurance (if it is collectible).

3

Liability Coverage

Section II of CA 00 01 contains the provisions relating to auto liability coverage. This section consists of the liability insuring agreement, coverage extensions, exclusions, and a provision concerning the limit of insurance.

The Insuring Agreement

There are three parts to the liability coverage insuring agreement.

The first part is the insurer's agreement to pay "all sums an insured legally must pay as damages because of bodily injury or property damage to which this insurance applies, caused by an accident and resulting from the ownership, maintenance or use of a covered auto." Although this statement seems straightforward, there are several terms and phrases in this agreement that deserve special attention.

The insuring agreement is the heart of the contract between the insurer and the insured. The first named insured is the party to which the insurer looks for payment of the policy premium; however, the term "the insured" is not limited to the payer of the premium. This section of CA 00 01 contains several clauses defining just who is an insured; an important classification, since any who qualify receive the benefits of the insuring agreement. It is also important to note that coverage under CA 00 01 applies *separately* to each insured seeking coverage or against whom a claim is made.

The insurer agrees to pay damages because of BI or PD "to which this insurance applies." This phrase is the insurer's round about way of telling the insured that, yes, he or she has insurance, but it does not apply to every single claim or lawsuit filed against the insured. There are exclusions in the policy that deny coverage to the insured under certain circumstances and the insured should be aware of that fact.

The liability insuring agreement notes that damages are covered if caused by an accident. The term "accident" is defined on the BAP, but that does not supersede the commonly accepted notion that the term centers on the unexpected and the unanticipated. In other words, the event that causes the bodily injury or property damage has to be unforeseen and unplanned on the part of the insured in order for the BAP to apply.

Finally, the insuring agreement applies to the ownership, maintenance, or use of a covered auto. Liability coverage applies to "covered autos" only and this is important for the insured to note. Only symbol 1 will make any auto a covered auto, so the insured needs to carefully choose which symbol is used to designate which covered auto. For example, if the insured has chosen symbol 2—owned autos only—as the designation for liability coverage, drives a nonowned auto on business purposes and has an at-fault accident, the BAP will not respond to any resulting claim or lawsuit.

The second part of the insuring agreement declares that the insurer will pay all sums that an insured must legally pay as a "covered pollution cost or expense." This is a defined term in the BAP and means "any cost or expense arising out of any request, demand, or order or any claim or suit by or on behalf of a governmental authority demanding that the insured or others test for, monitor, clean up, remove, contain, treat, detoxify or neutralize, or in any way respond to, or assess the effects of pollutants." The clause does give the insured some coverage for clean up costs, but that coverage is not unlimited.

The covered pollution cost or expense does not extend to instances in which the insured is delivering fuel oil or carrying waste products in its covered autos and then suffers an accident causing a spill onto the ground. However, there is coverage for spills or leaks from an auto part designed by its manufacturer to hold fuels, lubricants, or other fluids needed for the normal functioning of the covered auto; i.e., a gas tank or a radiator filled with antifreeze.

And, while the covered pollution cost or expense does not generally apply to the clean up of pollutants before such pollutants are put into the covered auto or after they are removed from the covered auto at their final destination, there is some coverage under certain circumstances. For example, if the insured's covered auto is on the property of a customer in order to pick up fuel oil for delivery and the auto backs into a tank containing the fuel oil, rupturing the tank and spilling it onto the ground, the insured's auto form will pay the clean up costs. The mandatory requirements here are that the accident must occur away from premises owned by or rented by the insured, the potential pollutants can not be in or upon the covered auto, the pollutant is upset or overturned as a result of the maintenance or use of a covered auto, and that the discharge or escape of the polluting substance(s) must be caused directly by that upset or overturn.

As a final limitation on this pollution clean up costs coverage, note that the insurer will pay only if there is either BI or PD to which the insurance applies that is caused by the same accident. The situation of the covered auto backing into and damaging the tank that is described above is an example. The accident caused property damage which subsequently caused the spillage; therefore, the insurer will pay for the clean up costs.

The third part of the insuring agreement deals with the insurer's duty to defend. Here the insurer agrees to defend any insured against a suit seeking damages or covered pollution cost or expense. Although it is widely accepted in legal and insurance circles that the duty to defend is broader than the duty to pay for damages, some courts went too far in interpreting this duty and ruled that since there was no statement limiting the duty to defend, the insurer had to defend the insured every time and under all circumstances. In reaction to this position, the BAP now contains the statement that the insurer has "no duty to defend any insured against a suit seeking damages for BI or PD or a covered pollution cost or expense to which this insurance does not apply." So, for example, if the lawsuit against the insured claims damage to property that the insured had in its care, custody, or control, such damage is not covered under liability exclusion 6. of the BAP and the insurer has no duty to defend the insured.

The insurer reserves to itself the right to investigate and settle any claim or lawsuit it considers appropriate. The insured, however, does not have the right to prevent a settlement even if he or she does not like the terms.

The last section of this duty to defend clause declares that the duty to defend or settle ends when the liability coverage limit of insurance has been exhausted by payment of judgments or settlements. It is important to note that the limits have to be exhausted by the payment of judgments or settlements; simply tendering the policy limits and walking away from the defense of the insured is not an acceptable way for the duty to defend to end.

When Does Duty to Defend End?

The claims department of an insurance company is split over the question of when their duty to defend ends. Some of the staff say that if an insurer tenders the policy limits for a claim, the duty to defend ends because the limits of liability on the policy have been exhausted. Others say that is not necessarily so and that an insurer can not just tend the policy limits to the court and walk away, leaving the insured to fend for himself.

The provision as to when the duty to defend ends should be considered as just a part of the entire duty to defend clause. The clause starts off with the insurer promising to defend any insured against a lawsuit; only after the insurer has made this promise does the issue of when the duty ends come into play. Simply tendering policy limits does not fulfill the promise to defend; it does not fulfill the promise of the clause taken as a whole. Besides, the wording of the phrase ties the ending of the duty to defend to

(scenario continues next page)

> *(continued from previous page)*
> using up the limits of the policy in the "payment of judgments or settlements." In other words, the insurer promises that the duty to defend ends only when the policy limits have been used up in the course of carrying out the obligation to settle a claim or lawsuit against the insured.

Who Is An Insured

There are several categories of insureds. The named insured is an insured for any covered auto. Regardless of whether the auto is owned or nonowned, private passenger type or other than private passenger type, as long as that auto is designated as a covered auto under the BAP, the named insured is an insured for liability coverage purposes. If the auto is not so designated, the named insured is not an insured even under his or her own BAP.

Anyone else using, with the named insured's permission, a covered auto owned, hired, or borrowed by the named insured is also considered an insured; however, note the following exceptions.

The owner or anyone else from whom the named insured hires or borrows a covered auto is not considered an insured. The insurer is mainly concerned with liability coverage for the named insured; if the named insured is hiring or borrowing another's auto, that other entity should have its own auto insurance.

An employee of the named insured is not an insured if the covered auto is owned by that employee or a member of his or her household. Here again, the named insured's insurer is trying to make the point that the owner of a hired or borrowed car should have his or her own car insurance that can apply should that owner need liability coverage.

Someone using a covered auto while working in the business of selling, servicing, repairing, parking or storing autos is not an insured unless that business belongs to the named insured. For example, if the named insured takes his car to a garage to be repaired and a garage employee takes the car for a test drive to check the repair work, that employee is not an insured under the named insured's policy should an accident occur. Liability coverage for that employee should come primarily from his employer's garage policy.

Anyone other than the named insured's employees, partners, or members (of a limited liability company) while moving property to or from a covered auto is not an insured. So, for example, if the named insured is delivering a heavy package to a customer and the customer's employee moves that package from the auto and, in doing so, drops the package onto the foot of a passerby, that employee is not an insured under the BAP if a claim is filed.

Likewise, a partner of the named insured or a member of the named insured's limited liability company is not an insured for a covered auto owned by him or her or a member of his or her household. Such autos can become covered autos under the BAP through the use of symbols 1 or 9, but the owners of the covered autos have to rely on their own policy for coverage—barring any endorsement to the BAP to the contrary.

Finally, anyone liable for the conduct of an insured is an insured, but only to the extent of that liability. This is something of an omnibus clause when it comes to granting the status of an insured under the BAP. It helps in cases where the lines of authority are blurred or when medium level supervisors are brought into a liability lawsuit. For example, if an employee of the named insured is sent by his or her immediate supervisor to deliver a package in a covered auto and that employee causes an accident, chances are the injured claimant will sue the employee, the supervisor, and the named insured. The BAP will offer a defense to the named insured because he or she is an insured for the use of any covered auto. The BAP will offer a defense to the employee because he or she is an insured by using a covered auto with the permission of the named insured. The supervisor could be left out in the cold were it not for this omnibus clause. The supervisor can be said to be liable for the conduct of the employee since the supervisor gave the order to the employee—something akin to the *respondeat superior theory*. Thus, this particular clause will make the supervisor an insured and the BAP will respond accordingly.

There are some additional points to make regarding who is an insured. The second clause—anyone while using with the named insured's permission a covered auto—requires permission from the named insured. For example, a thief who takes the named insured's car on a joyride is not a permittee and so, is not considered an insured. Additionally, the permittee has to be using a covered auto that the named insured owns, hires, or borrows; employers and employees alike should be aware that the BAP does not automatically make insureds out of employees who rent or borrow cars in their own names.

Coverage Extensions

This section of CA 00 01 includes supplementary payments provided by the insurer as well as out-of-state coverage extensions. The supplementary payments are in addition to the limit of insurance, so if the insurer makes any of these payments, it will not decrease the limits available for other claims or lawsuits brought against the insured.

These supplementary payments include: all the expenses incurred by the insurer; the cost of bail bonds (up to $2,000) required because of an accident; the cost of bonds to release attachments; all reasonable expenses incurred by the insured at the request of the insurer (including actual loss of earnings up to $250 a day for time off from work); all costs taxed against the insured in a lawsuit; and all interest on the full amount of any judgment that accrues after entry of the judgment.

The out-of-state coverage extensions are for covered autos while out of the state in which they are licensed. The insurer agrees to increase the limit of insurance for liability coverage to meet the limits specified by a compulsory or financial responsibility law of the jurisdiction where the covered auto is being used. For example, if a covered auto licensed in Mississippi (with liability coverage limits of $10,000 for BI) is being driven in Minnesota (where the required BI limit is $30,000), this coverage extension will guarantee the insured a $30,000 limit of insurance should an accident occur in Minnesota.

The second part of the coverage extension states that the insurer will provide the minimum amounts and types of coverages required of out-of-state vehicles by the jurisdiction where the covered auto is being used. For example, if the named insured is driving his or her covered auto in a state that requires no-fault coverage, the BAP will provide the required coverage to the named insured even if he or she does not have that coverage on the BAP.

Exclusions

There are 13 exclusions in the current CA 00 01 that curtail liability coverage.

Expected or Intended Injury

The first to consider is the expected or intended injury exclusion. It states that the insurer will not pay for BI or PD that is expected or intended from the standpoint of the insured. This seems simple enough. The liability insuring agreement applies to BI or PD caused by an accident; and the exclusion reinforces that point. However, in practice, this exclusion is difficult to use in order to deny a claim because of various legal interpretations.

If the insured intends to ram his car into another car and injure or kill the driver of the other car, the exclusion applies. But, if the insured intends to ram the other car but does not intend to injure the driver, is the exclusion applicable? Or, if the insured intends to ram the other car and hurt the driver but not as badly as it turns out, is the exclusion applicable? Courts around the country have struggled with this issue and the majority have developed a distinct difference between the act and the intent of that act. In other words, even if the act is intended by the insured, the exclusion will not apply unless the insurer can show that the insured also intended the resultant injury or damage.

In addition, there are other problems with the application of this particular exclusion. The question of whether the insured acted intentionally can be affected by factors such as intoxication, mental illness, or an assertion by the insured that he was acting in self defense. Note that the BAP does not make an exception for this exclusion based on self defense such as the CGL form does; but if the insured somehow uses his covered auto for self defense purposes, will the insurer really use the expected or intended exclusion to deny a bodily injury lawsuit made against the insured? Furthermore, can this exclusion be used to eliminate the minimum financial responsibility limits imposed by state law? If a state requires all drivers to carry a certain minimum level of tort liability insurance, this exclusion may not be allowed to circumvent that state law.

The bottom line for this exclusion is that, in theory, it makes good common sense because the insurance is supposed to apply to accidents; but, in practical terms, the use of this exclusion alone to deny coverage is leading from a weak position.

Contractual Exclusion

The contractual exclusion is the second one on the BAP. Any liability assumed under any contract or agreement is not covered by the BAP. There are, of course, exceptions. Liability assumed in an insured contract is covered, and liability that the insured would have in the absence of the contract or agreement is also covered. The term "insured contract" is defined in the BAP and this exclusion has to be considered in connection with the discussion of that definition in a later chapter. The second exception makes a contractual agreement irrelevant to the insured's liability coverage if the insured's own negligence causes the accident and damage.

Workers Compensation/Employers Liability Exclusion

Exclusions 3, 4, and 5 in the BAP deal with workers compensation and employee injury. The BAP will not pay for injuries already covered by workers compensation. Furthermore, if there is bodily injury to an employee of the insured arising out of and in the course of employment by the insured, or performing duties related to the insured's business, the BAP will not apply to those injuries. Finally, the BAP will not apply to BI to any fellow employee of the insured arising out of and in the course of employment.

These exclusions are based on the view that workers compensation and employers liability insurance are the proper methods of paying for injuries to employees hurt in the course of employment. The question that arises here is: what specifically does it mean to say that an injury must arise out of and in the course of employment? The BAP does not offer a definition and neither does the workers comp policy, so it has fallen to the courts to do so. "The test of the right to participate in the workers compensation fund is whether a causal connection existed between an employee's injury and his employment either through the activities, the conditions, or the environment of the employment."

This is a quote from an Ohio Supreme Court decision—*Bralle v. Daugherty* 61 Ohio St.2d 302 (1980)—and offers an example of the majority judicial opinion that workers comp payments require an employee to be injured as a result of his or her employment; simply put, the employment must cause the injury.

The fellow employee exclusion is worded so that if the working relationship between the employer and the employee is such that all are considered "fellow employees," the BAP will not apply to bodily injuries they suffer arising out of their employment. So, if the employee injures the employer, or vice versa, during the course of employment, the BAP will not cover those injuries.

The employers liability exclusion does not apply to bodily injury to domestic employees that are not entitled to workers comp benefits. A domestic employee is defined as "a person engaged in household or domestic work performed principally in connection with a residence premises," such as a maid or gardener. These people very often are not covered by the state workers compensation law and so, were they to be injured in an auto accident through the negligence of the insured, they would not be entitled to workers comp payments. In such a case, the insured's BAP would pay for the damages that the insured was legally obligated to pay. It is not meant to say that such payments are a substitute for workers compensation, in that any payments made under the BAP still have to be based on the fault of the insured; workers comp is, of course, no-fault coverage.

Finally, if the insured has assumed liability under an insured contract, the employers liability exclusion will not apply. This exception usually comes into play if the insured has leased a worker or has another's employees performing duties related to the insured's business; and, as part of that business arrangement, the insured has signed a contract or made an agreement with the other employer that he or she will assume employer's liability to an injured leased or borrowed employee. This exception reinforces the liability coverage afforded to the insured and preempts any possible conflict between the coverage afforded the insured under an insured contract and the employers liability exclusion. Note that this exception also dovetails with the wording on the employers liability insurance part of the workers comp policy that states that that insurance does not cover liability assumed under a contract. In essence, what the workers comp/employers liability policy takes away, the business auto coverage form gives back.

Care, Custody, or Control Exclusion

Exclusion 6 is the care, custody, or control exclusion. It applies to property damage to or covered pollution cost or expense involving property owned or transported by the insured or in the insured's care, custody, or control.

Property damage to property owned by the insured should not be covered under a liability policy; after all, the insured can not be liable to himself. Such coverage is more properly handled by a commercial property coverage form or an inland marine policy. An inland marine policy is also better for covering damage to property being transported by the insured.

Note that the exclusion applies to property in the insured's care, custody, or control. The wording here limits the applicability of the exclusion.

> **Employee-Caused Damage Within Insured's Care, Custody or Control?**
>
> *The insured's employee is moving an expensive painting from a customer's house into a covered auto. The employee drops the painting and damages it. The customer sues the insured employer and the employee over the damage and the insurer denies coverage based on the care, custody, or control exclusion. The insured's agent disputes the idea that the named insured had the painting in its care, custody, or control and wants coverage for his client.*
>
> The exclusion uses the term "the" when referring to the insured as opposed to "you," the named insured, or "an," which is a very general, inclusive word. If the insurer had worded the exclusion so that it applied to property in "your" care, custody, or control, the exclusion would have applied only to the named insured; in such a case, the employee would have coverage. Similarly, if the insurer had worded the exclusion thusly, "property in an insured's care, custody, or control," the exclusion would have applied to both the named insured and the employee since the word "an" means the exclusion applies if any insured had care, custody, or control.
>
> However, the insurer chose to have the exclusion apply to property in "the" insured's care, custody, or control. That word encompasses only the particular insured that had care, custody, or control at the time of the damage. In this example, the named insured is not that particular insured and so, the insurer owes the named insured, at the very least, a defense. And, if the named insured is held liable for the damage (which
>
> *(scenario continues next page)*

> *(continued from previous page)*
>
> is probable due to the *respondeat superior theory*), the insurer will pay. Unfortunately for the employee, he did have care, custody, and control at the time of the damage and the exclusion does apply to him.

Exclusions 7 and 8 are kin to exclusion 6 in that they address the handling of property. However, unlike exclusion 6, exclusions 7 and 8 apply to both bodily injury and property damage.

Handling of Property

Exclusion 7 precludes coverage for BI or PD resulting from the handling of property before it is moved from the place where it is accepted by the insured, or after it is moved from the covered auto to the place where it is finally delivered. This wording corresponds with the definition of "loading or unloading" found on the CGL form so that, if the insured has a CGL form and a BAP, he or she has liability coverage before moving property onto a covered auto, while the property is being loaded onto the auto, while the property is being transported on the covered auto, while the property is being unloaded from the auto, and after the property has been finally delivered. Either the CGL form or the BAP will respond to a liability claim from a third party based on the moving of property.

> ### Which Policy Covers - CGL or BAP?
>
> *An insured has both CGL and business auto policies for his small business. One day the insured picks up a sofa at a warehouse for delivery to a customer. As the sofa is being loaded onto the insured's truck he stumbles and accidentally knocks one of the warehouse employees off the loading dock onto the concrete below causing a minor injury. While the insured is confident that he has adequate liability coverage available through the two policies, he is not sure which policy will apply to this and any other losses that could occur throughout the pick up and delivery processes.*
>
> Which policy would apply to a claim depends on the circumstances of the claim. If the insured injures someone while walking into the warehouse before picking up the sofa, the CGL form would apply. If the insured picks up the sofa and injures someone while moving it to the covered auto, the BAP will respond. Similarly, if the insured is loading the sofa into the auto or unloading it from the auto and it falls onto a pedestrian causing injury, the BAP will respond to the BI claim. If the insured unloads the sofa and lets it rest on the sidewalk where someone trips over it, the BAP applies to the
>
> *(scenario continues next page)*

> *(continued from previous page)*
> resultant BI claim. If the insured is in the process of delivering the sofa but has not yet delivered it to its final resting place, and injures someone during that delivery, the BAP will apply to a BI claim. Only after delivering the sofa to its final resting place and walking away from the area can the insured rely on his CGL form to respond to a claim.

Movement of Property Exclusion

Exclusion 8 deals with the movement of property by mechanical device. The business auto policy will not cover BI or PD resulting from the movement of property by a mechanical device (other than a hand truck) unless the device is attached to the covered auto. For example, if the insured is using a hoist attached to a flatbed truck to load or unload bricks and someone is injured during that process, the BAP responds to the claim. If the insured is using a conveyor belt not attached to the truck or a forklift to unload the bricks and the bricks fall off the belt or forklift, injuring someone, exclusion 8 can be used to deny coverage under the BAP. The insured can look to his CGL form for coverage in that instance; as with exclusion 7, the wording in exclusion 8 corresponds with the wording of the "loading or unloading" definition on the CGL form to give the insured liability coverage in this particular instance under either the BAP or the CGL form.

Operation of Mobile Equipment Exclusion

Exclusion 9 on the BAP applies to BI or PD arising out of the operation of any equipment listed in paragraphs 6.b. and 6.c. of the definition of mobile equipment. These paragraphs describe equipment such as cherry pickers and similar devices used to raise or lower workers, air compressors, pumps, and generators. The definition of mobile equipment states that self-propelled vehicles with such equipment permanently attached are considered autos for coverage purposes, but exclusion 9 attempts to make clear that the operation of the equipment itself is not covered under the auto policy. For example, if the insured has a cherry picker mounted on a covered auto, the BAP will cover the over-the-road hazards of driving the auto from one work site to another. If, however, while the cherry picker is being used, it hits and injures a pedestrian or smashes into a car or building and causes property damage, the BAP will not cover the resulting claim. The CGL form complements the auto policy by covering such an equipment exposure and excluding the vehicle exposure.

Note that there is a new endorsement, CA 00 51, that expands this exclusion. CA 00 51 (with an edition date of December, 2004) says the BAP liability insurance does not apply to the following: BI, PD or covered pollution cost or expense arising out of the operation of any equipment listed in paragraphs 6.b. and 6.c. of the definition of mobile equipment; or machinery or equipment that is on, attached to, or part of, a land vehicle that would qualify under the definition of mobile equipment, if it were not subject to a compulsory or financial responsibility law where it is licensed or principally garaged. This is a new endorsement that applies to the business auto coverage form, the motor carrier coverage form, and the truckers coverage form. It is discussed further in Chapter 11 of this book.

Completed Operations Exclusion

Exclusion 10 relates to BI or PD arising out of the named insured's work after that work has been completed or abandoned. Whether a completed operations exposure can result from the ownership, maintenance, or use of an auto is not clear, but the bottom line is that such an exposure is not covered by the auto policy. Note that the wording of the exclusion tracks closely with the definition of products-completed operations hazard in the CGL form, and this strengthens the point that a completed operations claim should be handled under the CGL form and not the auto policy.

Pollution Exclusion

The pollution hazard is considered in exclusion 11. The wording of the pollution exclusion makes it just about a total ban on any coverage for a pollution incident. Coverage for BI or PD arising out of the discharge or release or escape of pollutants is excluded: when the pollutants are being transported or handled or in the course of transit, or being stored or processed in or upon the covered auto, or before the pollutants are moved into a covered auto, or after the pollutants are moved from the covered auto to the place where they are finally disposed of or delivered. In other words, any exposure, from before being moved onto a covered auto, through transit on the covered auto, and on to final disposition of the pollutants, is excluded under the BAP. Any exposure, that is, but for those included in the exceptions to the exclusion.

That part of the pollution exclusion that deals with pollutants being transported or handled or stored or processed in or upon a covered auto has an exception that allows coverage for BI or PD arising out of the release or discharge of pollutants (such as, fuels, lubricants, fluids) directly from an auto part designed by the manufacturer to hold or store such pollutants (e.g., gas tank, radiator).

Both the part of the pollution exclusion that deals with pollutants before they are accepted by the insured for movement onto a covered auto and the part that deals with pollutants after they are moved from the covered auto to their final disposition have an exception. Namely, there is BI and PD coverage under the BAP if a release or discharge of pollutants occurs away from the insured's premises and is caused directly by upset, overturn, or damage as a result of the maintenance or use of a covered auto.

For example, if one of the named insured's covered autos (not carrying potential pollutants) collides with a tanker truck on the highway causing the (tanker) truck's cargo to spill and pollute the soil. Any resulting claim for bodily injury or property damage for which the insured is held liable will be covered under the BAP. The pollution exclusion under the BAP applies when the pollutants are being transported or moved by the insured in a covered auto.

To illustrate the exception to this exclusion: suppose an employee of the named insured, driving a covered auto, is involved in an at-fault accident. The crankcase of the covered auto is ruptured and oil seeps out, creating a slick on the roadway. Moments later, another auto comes along, slips on the oil slick, and crashes. If the named insured is held liable for injury and damage resulting from the other car slipping on the oil slick, the pollution exclusion on the insured's BAP will not apply. The oil was for the normal mechanical functioning of the covered auto and escaped from an auto part designed to hold the oil.

Finally, suppose the insured has delivered a hazardous cargo of pollutants to his customer without incident. While attempting to drive off the customer's lot, the insured accidentally backs his covered auto into a tank where the pollutants are stored, toppling the tank and causing the pollutants to spill out, injuring the customer's employees. The pollutants were "finally delivered" by the insured, but the exception to the exclusion—accident occurring away from the premises of the insured, involving pollutants not in or upon a covered auto being released due to the direct use of a covered auto—means that the BAP will respond to claims for injuries made against the insured.

In addition to the exceptions in the pollution exclusion, it is interesting to note that the exclusion does not mention clean up costs. The CGL form clearly excludes loss, cost, or expense arising out of any request or demand or order to clean up pollutants; however, such language is not part of the pollution exclusion found on the BAP. Does this mean that the BAP will pay clean up costs? The answer to this question is found in the liability insuring agreement wherein the insurer promises to pay covered pollution costs or expenses.

A "covered pollution cost or expense" is a defined term on the BAP (and will be discussed in more detail in a later chapter of this book) meaning "any cost or expense arising out of any request, demand, or order, or any claim or suit by or on behalf of a governmental authority demanding that the insured test for, monitor, clean up ... or in any way respond to ... the effects of pollutants." In short, the business auto policy will pay clean up costs, but be aware that such coverage is limited in its scope.

The insurer will pay for covered pollution cost or expense only if there is either bodily injury or property damage caused by an accident that the BAP covers. In other words, unless the pollution spill or release is caused by the same accident that also causes some BI or PD that the auto policy covers, the insurer will not pay clean up costs. For example, if the insured is transporting potential pollutants in a covered auto and has an at-fault accident, causing a spill onto the roadway, the insurer will not pay for the clean up costs because such an accident causing BI or PD is excluded by the pollution exclusion. On the other hand, if in that same accident, the insured damaged another person's auto and gasoline from that auto's gas tank (or the covered auto's gas tank) leaked out onto the pavement and surrounding property, the BAP would respond and pay for the clean up costs because that type of leak is not excluded by the pollution exclusion.

The limitation on the scope of the clean up costs coverage is reinforced by the insurer in the definition of "covered pollution cost or expense". That definition includes the wording of the BAP's pollution exclusion in order to let the insured know just what "covered pollution cost or expense" does not include. If the clean up cost or expense arises out of a discharge or release or escape of pollutants that is encompassed by the pollution exclusion, the insurer will deny coverage.

War Exclusion

The war exclusion on the BAP is similar to the one on the CGL form and other typical insurance policies. BI or PD due to war or any act or condition incident to war is not covered under the auto policy. The exclusion applies only to liability assumed under a contract or agreement. The presence of this exclusion in the business auto policy is greeted mainly by a "who cares" attitude; this is not an auto policy exclusion that many people have legal disputes over.

Racing Exclusion

The final exclusion on the business auto form, CA 00 01, applies to racing exposures. The insurance does not apply to covered autos while used in any professional or organized racing or demolition contest or stunting activity, or while practicing for such contest or activity. Such activities and contests are high risk exposures that should be insured under specialty lines policies.

Limit of Insurance

This part of the liability coverage section of the BAP emphasizes that, regardless of the number of covered autos, insureds, premiums paid, claims made, or vehicles involved in an accident, the most the insurer will pay is the liability limit shown in the declarations. The amount paid for the total of all damages and covered pollution cost or expense combined can not exceed the limit stated in the declarations.

As an illustration, if the insured has three covered autos and all are involved in the same accident, the insured has the declared limits of liability available to him, not three times the limit. If there are twenty people hurt in that accident, the insured has the declared limits of liability available to him, not twenty times the limit. This clause acts as an anti-stacking provision.

And to counter a possible stacking issue, this clause also declares that no one will be entitled to receive duplicate payments for the same elements of loss under the auto policy and any med pay coverage, uninsured motorists coverage, or underinsured motorists coverage. All these coverages are separate in form and in intent and this clause serves to clarify the separation.

4

Physical Damage Coverage

Section III of the Business Auto Coverage Form is the physical damage coverage part of the Business Auto Policy. It consists of the coverage agreements, a coverage extension, exclusions, limit of insurance information, and a deductible provision.

The Coverage Agreements

The coverage agreements in the physical damage section of the BAP list the various ways in which a covered auto can suffer physical damage. The insurer agrees to pay for loss to a covered auto or its equipment under comprehensive coverage, specified causes of loss coverage, or collision coverage. To activate coverage a covered auto designation symbol(s) must be placed in item two of the declarations form beside the coverage(s) that the insured has chosen. For example, if the insured wants collision coverage on owned autos only, symbol 2 must appear in the column next to collision coverage on the declarations form. If the insured wants comprehensive and collision coverages on any auto, symbol 1 must appear in the column next to the comprehensive coverage and the collision coverage. Regardless of the coverage(s) chosen, there must be a covered auto designation symbol(s) listed in item two of the declarations form in order for the coverage(s) to be in effect.

The insuring agreement under section III of the BAP states that the insurer will pay for a "loss." "Loss" is defined by the policy as a direct and accidental loss or damage to a covered auto. In other words, the covered auto has to suffer direct physical damage; there is no consequential damage or loss of use damage coverage.

The covered auto and its equipment are covered for loss. The covered auto is easy to identify in that the designation symbols are used for that purpose. A question can arise, though, over just what "equipment" includes. The BAP does not define the term, so it falls to common sense to provide interpretive guidelines. A covered auto's equipment includes such things as the jack, spare tire, or any item that is part of the auto (except those items specifically excluded). "Equipment" does not include the insured's clothes, transistor radios, eyeglasses, or any item not commonly accepted as being part of an auto. The bottom line is that although the definition of equipment is open to interpretation (especially by a court), common sense has to be used in deciding whether an item can be considered a covered auto's "equipment."

As noted previously, the covered causes of loss are comprehensive, specified, or collision. Comprehensive coverage is for loss from any cause except collision. Specified causes of loss are spelled out on the policy: fire, lightning, explosion, theft, windstorm, hail, earthquake, flood, mischief or vandalism, or the sinking, burning, collision, or derailment of any conveyance transporting the covered auto. Collision coverage is for loss caused by the covered auto's collision with another object or its overturn.

If the insured has chosen specified causes of loss coverage, the covered auto must suffer loss by one or more of the causes specified in order for the coverage to apply. If questions arise, they usually revolve around the issue of comprehensive versus collision coverage. Just where is the dividing line between a comprehensive loss and a collision loss? Some examples may help in the discussion.

What is Collision?

Suppose a covered auto is parked on the street. A biker, distracted by some noise, runs into the covered auto and damages it. The insurer of the covered auto wonders if this is a collision loss since the auto was not moving at the time of loss.

The loss is a collision loss. There is no requirement that the covered auto be in motion or that the collision be with another auto, just another "object."

A covered auto came into contact with a large hole in the road causing the frame to break on both sides. The question arose over whether the roadbed is an object so that damaging contact with it is covered as a collision loss.

In *Welch v. Western Casualty and Surety Company*, 567 S.W.2d 743 (1978), a Missouri court of appeals decided that collision means any striking together or against and does not necessarily connote any particular degree of force.

(scenario continues next page)

> *(continued from previous page)*
>
> The court noted other legal authority that a chasm, hole, rut, or other declivity in the roadway can be considered another object. And, the court implied that the size of this particular hole made it, in the court's opinion, "another object." For these reasons, the Missouri court held that collision was the proximate cause of the loss.

The following examples may also help clarify just what is a collision loss:

- A covered auto, parked on the street, is damaged by a drunk driver.
- A covered auto is parked on a hill and a child enters the car and releases the parking brake, allowing the auto to roll down the hill and hit a tree.
- A covered auto is stolen by a mentally unstable person, driven at high speed, and crashes into another car.

The connecting thread in all three of these examples is the question of whether such losses are by collision or by vandalism.

If the insurer wants to claim such losses are by vandalism, it has the burden of proving that point. However, the legal essence of vandalism and malicious mischief requires a *willful intent* to cause damage and so, proving vandalism or malicious mischief may be difficult under conditions such as those given in the examples.

Deciding whether a loss is due to collision or a comprehensive cause of loss can be difficult in some circumstances. However, due to the lack of a definition of collision in the BAP, the insured must always get the benefit of any doubt.

Towing

As part of the physical damage coverage agreement, the insurer also agrees to pay up to the limit shown in the declarations for towing and labor costs incurred each time a covered private passenger auto is disabled. The labor must be performed at the place of disablement.

There are several important points to emphasize in relation to towing coverage:

- The towing coverage is set before a claim arises; if the insured chooses $100 of coverage, then that is the most the insurer will pay for any towing. The costs are for each time a covered auto is disabled; if the insured has his or her auto break down five times in

a week and has to have the auto towed each time, the insured has at least the chosen coverage amount of $100 available for each tow.
- The covered auto must be of the private passenger type. The commercial lines manual (CLM) defines a private passenger auto as "a four wheel auto of the private passenger or station wagon type," with pickups, panel trucks, and vans not used for business being rated as private passenger autos. Granted, the business auto policy itself does not define a "private passenger type" auto, but a distinction is meant to be made between private passenger autos and trucks and semi-trailers. The insurer, through the wording of this towing clause, intends to cover private passenger type autos only and can be expected to resist towing costs for any other type of auto.
- Labor costs are covered only for the labor performed at the place of disablement. If the insured has a covered auto towed to a garage where repairs are performed, the labor costs of the repairs at the garage are not covered under the towing clause.

Labor Costs

The insured parked his covered auto in a customer's lot and when he came out to start the car, it would not start. The insured called a garage and requested a tow. When the repairman arrived on the scene, he told the insured that only a jump for the battery was needed. The jump was made, the car started, and the insured left. He submitted the bill for the jump to the insurer and it was denied since no towing was done and the insurer said any labor costs had to be in connection with towing to be covered.

The insurer is incorrect. The towing agreement clearly states that the insurer will "pay up to the limit shown ... for towing and labor costs incurred each time a covered auto ... is disabled". The labor costs are tied to the disablement of the covered auto and not the towing. If the car can be started and made to run without a tow, the towing clause on the BAP will still pay for the labor costs involved. The car was disabled and the labor was performed at the place of disablement; therefore, the insurer should pay the bill. Besides, a jump is cheaper than a tow and the insurer should be glad it has a lower bill to pay since without the jump, a tow certainly would have been required.

Glass Breakage

The insurer agrees to pay for the following losses under comprehensive coverage if the named insured carries such coverage on the covered auto: glass breakage, loss caused by hitting a bird or animal, and loss caused by falling objects or missiles. The insured has the option of having glass breakage caused by a covered auto's collision or overturn considered a loss under collision coverage.

This agreement works to the advantage of the insured if he or she has no collision coverage, or if the insured has collision coverage and comprehensive coverage, but with a higher deductible on the collision coverage. Of course, if the insured has collision coverage but not comprehensive coverage, these types of losses could still be covered as collision losses.

The purpose of this particular clause is not too clear. Perhaps since ISO includes these types of losses in the other than collision category on the personal auto policy, it was thought that the business auto policy ought to state something similar. If the covered auto suffers these types of losses, this clause does help clarify how the insurer wants to cover such losses; but, as noted, these types of losses could still be considered collision losses if the insured has no other type of physical damage coverage.

Coverage Extension

The BAP contains a coverage extension that covers temporary transportation expenses of the named insured due to the theft of a covered auto; that is, expenses incurred by the insured if he or she has to rent or borrow or hire a car because his or her covered auto has been stolen. The insurer agrees to pay up to $20 per day for this coverage extension to a maximum of $600. This extension is for no more than 30 days coverage.

This limited coverage is available only under the following conditions: the loss has to be due to the theft of the covered auto; the covered auto has to be of the private passenger type; and, the covered auto has to have either comprehensive or specified causes of loss coverage. If, for example, the covered auto has only collision coverage and is damaged in a collision with another car and can not be used, this extension will not pay for temporary transportation expenses for the insured. Note, though, that the scope of this extension can be expanded through the use of an endorsement (CA 99 23) so that the expenses incurred for the rental of an auto due to loss (any direct or accidental loss or damage) to a covered auto will be paid.

This coverage extension does not have a monetary deductible applied to it, but there is a waiting period before it does apply. The insurer will pay for temporary transportation expenses incurred during the period beginning 48 hours after the theft and ending (regardless of the policy's expiration) when the covered auto is returned to use, the insurer pays for its loss, or when the maximum of $600 is met. So, if the insured must rent a temporary car immediately after the theft of the covered auto, the cost for that rental for the first 48 hours will not be paid under this coverage extension. Likewise, if the rental expenses continue for more than 30 days ($20 x 30 days = $600), the insured is on his or her own.

The coverage extension also applies to loss of use expenses. The BAP now will pay the expenses for which an insured becomes legally responsible to pay for the loss of use of a vehicle rented or hired under a written rental contract. As an example: the insured rents a car and agrees to be responsible for the loss of use expenses if an accident occurs; subsequently, the insured has a collision and the rental car is out of commission for a week. The insured's BAP will pay the rental agency's loss of use expense claim.

This coverage is not automatic. The coverage is for hired auto physical damage. The insured has to have accepted responsibility for the loss of use expenses under a written rental contract, and the expenses are paid if the loss is caused by a cause of loss that the insured has chosen for his covered auto. As an example of this last requirement, the loss of use expenses are paid after an other than collision loss if the insured has chosen this type of coverage for his covered autos. If the insured has collision coverage only on his BAP, and a hired car is damaged by a fire or by vandals, the policy will not pay for the loss of use expenses. This is so even if the insured has contracted to pay for the expenses under the terms of the rental agreement.

The most that the insurer will pay for any expenses for loss of use is $20 per day, to a maximum of $600.

Physical Damage Exclusions

The BAP has five main exclusions that apply to the physical damage section.

The first one deals with loss caused by or resulting from nuclear hazard or war. These are the standard nuclear and war exclusions and they apply regardless of any other cause or event that contributes concurrently or in any sequence to the loss.

The second exclusion can be seen in combination with the exclusion under the liability coverage section of the BAP that applies to racing. Just as the liability exclusion denies coverage for BI and PD due to the covered autos being used in races or demolition or stunting contests, the second exclusion under the physical damage section of the BAP denies coverage for loss to any covered auto while used in any professional or organized racing or demolition contest or stunting activity. If the insured wants coverage for these types of exposures, there are specialty markets for that.

Exclusion three is the wear and tear exclusion. The insurer will not pay for loss caused by wear and tear, freezing, mechanical or electrical breakdown; also excluded are losses caused by blowouts, punctures, or other road damage to tires. This exclusion is limited in that it does not apply if these causes of loss are themselves caused by another loss that is covered by the BAP. For example, if an auto with comprehensive coverage is stolen and later recovered with a burned out clutch and brakes, the wear and tear on the auto can be attributed to the theft and therefore, will be covered. As another example, if electrical circuitry found in the dashboard area of the covered auto is damaged as a result of a covered collision, this particular exclusion will not apply to the electrical breakdown. Another example: if the covered auto's tires are slashed by vandals, the loss is not subject to the puncture exclusion if the insured has comprehensive or specified causes of loss coverage.

> **Application of Wear & Tear Exclusion**
>
> *The insured went away for the weekend and left his covered auto with the battery charging for three days. When he returned, the battery had over-charged and battery acid had mixed with the gasoline, changing into sulfuric acid. The fumes contaminated the entire vehicle and the car was unusable because the sulfuric acid caused skin irritation when a person got close to the car. Also, all the metal on the car turned green. The insured submitted a claim and the insurer denied coverage, citing the wear and tear exclusion and the mechanical or electrical exclusion.*
>
> The exclusion does not apply in this instance. Even though the wear and tear on the battery over a period of time caused it to lose and fail to keep its charge, this wear and tear was not the direct cause of the claimed loss. The direct cause of the loss was accidentally putting more electricity into the battery than it could hold. Furthermore, the creation of the sulfuric acid fumes from acid overflowing the battery is not the mechanical or electrical breakdown referred to in the exclusion. That phrase refers to damage caused by wire connections separating or by the friction of wires rubbing together, leading to broken or short circuits.

The fourth exclusion deals with loss to electronic equipment in the covered auto including audio, visual, or data electronic devices, and radar detection equipment. Audio and visual electronic devices also include tapes and compact discs. The exclusion wording dealing with electronic equipment and audio and visual electronic devices is in the policy because of the high risk of loss, mainly through theft. Electronic equipment is defined as equipment "that receives or transmits audio, visual, or data signals and that is not designed solely for the reproduction of sound." The radar detection equipment exclusion is in the policy obviously because the insurer does not want to encourage speeding and because the use of such items is illegal in some states and the insurer does not want to be accused of assisting in an illegal act.

Such equipment can be insured against loss under the BAP if endorsements are used; the premiums for these endorsements are meant to account for the high exposure to loss. However, the BAP itself offers certain exceptions to the exclusion.

The electronic equipment exclusion is not applicable to equipment designed solely for the reproduction of sound (e.g. radios, tape decks, compact disc players), provided such equipment is permanently installed in the covered auto at the time of loss; or, such equipment is removable from a housing unit that is permanently installed in the covered auto at the time of loss. Also, the equipment has to be designed to be solely operated by use of the power from the auto's electrical system.

The most contested issue in this exception is the meaning of "permanently installed." Since there is no definition in the policy, any dispute will be handled by a court on a case by case basis.

When Is Electronic Equipment Permanently Installed?

The insured had a citizens band radio and a scanner bolted to brackets which in turn were bolted to the underside of the dashboard of the insured's covered auto. After the items were stolen, the insured put in a claim which was subsequently denied by the insurer. The insurer said the items were not permanently installed since the equipment could be easily removed from the car if it were sold. The insured claims the items were permanently installed in his opinion and should be covered.

The phrase "permanently installed" is a relative term. The fifth edition of Black's Legal Dictionary describes "permanent" as fixed or intended to be fixed, but not intended to always be perpetual. A New York appeals court in *Troncillito v. Farm Family Mutual Insurance Company*, 406 N.Y.S.3d 143 (1978) stated that the important factor in an instance like this is the insured's intent to keep the equipment installed in the car for as long as he owns it. Therefore, permanency seems to hinge on intent and it is the insured's intent that counts. Most people own a car for only a few years and the word "permanent" must be considered in light of that limited period of time; so, if the insured installs an item with the intention that it remain in the auto until it is removed by the insured, that item is permanently installed.

Another exception to this electronic equipment exclusion is for equipment that is necessary for the normal operation of the covered auto, the monitoring of the operating system, or equipment that is an integral part of the unit housing any sound reproduction equipment permanently installed in the opening of the dash or console of the covered auto normally used by the manufacturer for installation of a radio. This exception is meant for the modern day auto that uses computer modules to operate the car and its components, to tell the driver if his seat belt is not fastened, if the oil is low, or if the lights are on. This type of electrical equipment is an integral part of the auto, helping it to operate as the piece of machinery it was built to be. As such, a loss to this type of equipment is a loss to the auto itself and can not in practical terms be excluded from coverage.

The BAP also has an exclusion pertaining to the issue of diminution in value (that is, where the insured claims that the auto is worth less in its wrecked but repaired condition than if it had not been wrecked, using the argument that the auto is now going to be worth less at resale time.) The insurer will not pay for loss to a covered auto due to diminution in value.

The term "diminution in value" is defined on the BAP as the actual or perceived loss in market value or resale value which results from a direct and accidental loss. It is no secret that a car that has been damaged in an accident has a market value that is less than it was prior to the accident, even if the car has been completely repaired. Some have argued that this loss in value is part of the physical damage and should be covered by the auto policy. However, this argument does not recognize several points. Physical damage coverage applies to direct loss to a covered auto; diminution in value is a consequential loss. Also, an exact loss in market value cannot be easily and objectively established; this would affect any loss payment and complicate attempts to establish a proper premium to cover that loss exposure.

Some courts are of the opinion that when the auto policy does not specifically address the diminution in value question, it is a covered loss; for example, see *State Farm Mutual Automobile insurance Company v. Mabry*, 556 S.E.2d 114 (Ga. 2001). The diminution in value exclusion should clarify the intent of the policy to not cover that particular exposure.

Limit of Insurance

This clause gives the insurer options on how to pay for a loss to a covered auto. The insurer can either pay the actual cash value of the damaged or stolen property at the time of loss; or it can pay the cost of repairing or replacing the damaged or stolen property with other property of like kind and quality. In either case, whichever option costs less is the one the insurer will choose.

If the insurer chooses to pay the actual cash value (ACV) of the damaged or stolen property, such value will be decided as of the time of loss. In other words, if the insured paid $8,000 for his auto in December, 2002 and suffers a loss to the car in June, 2004, the amount paid for the loss will reflect the June, 2004 value and not the amount paid for the car by the insured.

Furthermore, an adjustment for depreciation and physical condition will be made in determining actual cash value in the event of a total loss. For example of how the physical condition adjustment is made, say the insured has a 1998 Saturn that has over 200,000 miles on the odometer and quite a few dents and rust marks on the body of the car. The insurer will take these physical conditions into account before paying the insured for the total loss of his car. This action on the part of an insurer is simply a recognition of the fact that a much used and abused car just does not have the same actual cash value as that of a well maintained, dent-free, and low mileage vehicle. As for depreciation, all cars depreciate in value over time, and recognition of this is part of the legal contract between the insured and the insurer.

If the insurer chooses to repair or replace the damaged or stolen property, the replacement parts or items have to be of like kind and quality. This is not to say that the insured will receive the same parts or items that he or she lost, but the quality has to be the same. For example, if the insured loses a brand name engine part that costs $400 that can be replaced with a lesser known brand (but equally efficient part) that costs $350, the insured will get the $350 part. The insurer is not trying to cheat the insured with these provisions, but is simply trying to put the insured back in the same position he was in prior to the loss. The purpose of this physical damage insurance is to make the insured "whole", to make him as he was before the loss and not to enrich or make him better off than before the loss.

The limit of insurance clause also makes the insured aware of the fact that the auto policy will not pay for betterment in the event of a partial loss. Betterment is an improvement that adds to the value of a piece of property. However, the auto policy does not specifically define betterment, and this can lead to a dispute over the amount of payment for a loss.

For example, due to a covered loss, the insured had to have his car's engine rebuilt. The total cost of the repair work was $2,000. The damaged engine had 75,000 miles of use. The insurer took the position that the average life span of an auto engine is 100,000, so it applied a betterment penalty of 75% to the repair work cost. The insurer decided that the insured had used up 75% of the engine's life and that to pay the full amount of the repair cost would be to give the insured this 75% back; in other words, a betterment. The insured received 25% of the $2,000, or $500 (less the deductible, of course).

Another example: the insured has a used piece of equipment on the covered auto. The equipment is damaged in a covered collision loss and has to be replaced. The used part cost $500; the replacement part costs $600. The replacement piece costs more than the used piece since the equipment manufacturer makes only "new and improved" parts now. The insurer would pay for the replacement part, but only at the old, used cost of $500. The $100 betterment amount will not be paid.

Both examples would leave the average insured wondering what happened to his insurance coverage.

The theory supporting the betterment provision is that it reinforces the principle of indemnity. Namely, an insurance payment should put an insured back in the same position as prior to the covered loss; if the payment would better his position, insurance should not pay for that betterment. A problem arises, though, when an insurer contends that any new part added to a car after a loss constitutes betterment. This is not really an automatic fact; after all, if a car is ten years old but has a new radiator installed after a collision, the market value of the car is not really increased. It would be more appropriate if insurers considered as betterment only that which betters (increases) the value of the entire car, as opposed to just that of individual parts. Or perhaps, the insurer could define betterment on the policy. Either way would improve the insured's understanding of the loss payment process.

Deductibles

The deductible is the portion the insured must pay in the event of a loss. For example, if the insured has collision coverage for his or her covered auto and has chosen a $500 deductible, that means that the insured will pay for the first $500 in damage; the insurer will pay the remainder only after that $500 amount is exceeded.

The deductibles are listed on the declarations form and apply to whichever coverage the insured has chosen: comprehensive, specified causes of loss, and/or collision. The deductibles apply to each covered auto and not to each occurrence. This means that if the insured has 20 covered autos, each auto has a deductible and if they each suffer a loss at the same time (e.g., because of a hail storm or flood), the insured is facing 20 deductibles.

Any comprehensive coverage deductible does not apply to loss caused by fire or lightning. The insurer will pay for such losses from dollar one. Also, the declarations form notes that if the insured has specified causes of loss coverage, the only deductible is a $25 deductible for each covered auto for loss caused by mischief or vandalism.

5

Business Auto Conditions

The conditions section of the business auto policy consists of five loss conditions and eight general conditions. And, as with other ISO coverage forms for other commercial lines, the common policy conditions form, IL 00 17, is added to the BAP for a complete coverage part.

Loss Conditions

Appraisal

The first loss condition on the BAP deals with appraisal for physical damage loss. If the named insured and the insurer disagree on the amount of loss, either party may demand an appraisal, with each party selecting an appraiser. A call for an appraisal can come from either the insured or the insurer with neither party requiring the approval of the other in order for the appraisal process to begin.

The two appraisers then choose a "competent and impartial" umpire. The umpire will look over the appraisals submitted by the two parties and side with one or the other; a decision agreed to by any two will be binding on all.

Note that each party pays its chosen appraiser and each bears the expenses of the appraisal process and the umpire equally.

This procedure may lead an insured to believe that once it has won over the umpire to its evaluation of the loss, it will receive a check from the insurer quickly. Not necessarily. The insurer goes on to declare in this condition that even if it submits to an appraisal, it still retains the right to deny the claim. If the insurer has a reason to deny coverage, it will do so; an agreement on the value of the loss simply means that that is the amount the insurer will eventually pay if it agrees that the loss is a covered one.

Duties in the Event of Loss

The second loss condition lists the duties of the insured in the event of an accident, claim, lawsuit, or loss. The insurer begins this condition with a warning: it has no duty to provide coverage under the policy unless there has been full compliance with the listed duties. The insurer is stating that if the insured ignores its duties after a loss or claim, the insurer may very well deny coverage. For example, if the insured will not cooperate with the insurer in the investigation of an accident by declining to relate pertinent details of the accident, the insurer has reserved for itself the right to deny coverage. As another example, if the insured has an accident and pays for the injuries and damages of the accident victim out of his own pocket and then presents a bill to the insurer, the insurer can deny any coverage.

The insurer is basing its position on the idea that the BAP is a contractual agreement and if one party to that contract (the insured) breaches the conditions of the agreement, then the other party (the insurer) is justified in voiding the contract. The insurer is claiming its situation in the loss is prejudiced by the actions or inaction of the insured to the extent that it can not properly defend against a lawsuit or fairly settle a claim. And, it is the issue of prejudice that will be the ultimate factor in deciding whether an insurer can use a breach by the insured of the duties after an accident or loss to deny coverage. To what extent does the insurer have to be prejudiced in order to justifiably deny a claim?

Unfortunately, there is no judicial unanimity here. For example, in *Mount Vernon Fire Insurance Company v. DLRH Associates* 967 F. Supp. 105 (S.D.N.Y. 1997), a federal district court found that "the right of an insurer to receive notice has been held to be so fundamental that the insurer need not show prejudice to be able to disclaim liability." On the other hand, in *Cooperative Fire Insurance Ass. Of Vermont v. White Caps, Inc.* 694 A.2d 34 (Vt. 1997), the Supreme Court of Vermont decided that a breach of the notice condition must result in substantial prejudice to the insurer before coverage can be denied. So basically, if an insurer denies coverage due to the insured's failure to comply with the duties after a loss condition, whether that denial will stand depends on the facts of the instant case and the court that hears the evidence.

In any case, some of the duties of the insured are: give the insurer prompt notice of the accident or loss; immediately send copies of notices or legal papers to the insurer; cooperate with the investigation of the claim and defense against the suit; assume no obligations and make no payments without the insurer's consent; promptly notify the police if the covered auto is stolen; take all reasonable steps to protect the covered auto from further damage; and permit the insurer to inspect the covered auto proving the loss before its repair.

The insured should note that he or she must take all reasonable steps to protect the covered auto from further damage; and the insured should further note that the insurer declares that the insured should keep a record of expenses "for consideration in the settlement of the claim". Just what constitutes "reasonable steps" and what is meant by keeping a record of expenses "for consideration in the settlement" is not spelled out in the policy. Perhaps the insurer is saying that it will consider whether to pay the expenses, but does not automatically agree to pay them unless, for example, the insurer deems the expenses as reasonable, regardless of what the insured believes. In most cases, the insurer would probably repay the insured for such expenses without any hassles, but the expenses should be reasonable and documented. The insured should be pro-active in this area and keep the insurer informed of his or her actions, and make sure such actions are approved by the insurer in advance.

Legal Action Against the Insurer

The third loss condition addresses legal action against the insurer. No one may bring legal action against the insurer under the BAP until there has been full compliance with all the terms of the auto policy; and, until the insurer agrees in writing that the insured has an obligation to pay a liability claim. This condition allows the insurer to control the processing of a claim, in that the insurer does not want to allow the insured (or anyone else) to try to force the payment of a claim through a lawsuit before the legal liability of the insured has been established or before the actual cost of physical damage to a covered auto has been established.

This condition goes on to state that no one has the right under the BAP to bring the insurer into an action to determine the insured's liability. This emphasizes the point that the BAP is an agreement between the insured and the insurer. If there is a question about the insured's legal liability for injury or damage, that is an issue between the insured and the claimant; the insurer is not supposed to be sued to determine the insured's liability. However, some jurisdictions may have statutes allowing a third party claimant to name both the insured and the insurer in a lawsuit, and if so, such statutes overrule this condition.

Loss Payment

The fourth loss condition gives the insurer options of how to handle payments for physical damage to covered autos. The insured may have an accident from a covered cause of loss and think he or she will automatically be paid in cash for the damage done to the auto. Not so. The loss payment clause gives the insurer the option of: paying for, repairing or replacing damaged or stolen property; returning stolen property; or taking all or any part of the damaged or stolen property at an agreed or appraised value.

The first option corresponds with the limit of insurance clause under the physical damage coverage section of the BAP. In that clause, the insurer states that the most it will pay for loss is the lesser of the ACV of the damaged or stolen property or the cost of repairing or replacing the damaged or stolen property. The loss payment loss condition officially gives the insurer (and notifies the insured of) the option of paying for the loss or repairing or replacing the damaged property.

The second option allows the insurer to return the stolen property instead of paying for it; however, the insurer will make some payments. The insurer will pay for the expense of returning the property—e.g. if the car has been taken into another state and then found, it will pay to have the car returned to the insured either by tow truck or by hiring a driver. And, if the auto has been damaged after the theft, the insurer will pay for that damage. For example, if a thief steals the covered auto and then crashes it into a tree and abandons it, the insurer will pay for the collision damage first and then return the auto to the insured.

The third option allows the insurer to take all or part of the damaged or stolen property at an agreed upon or appraised value. This option makes the point that the insurer may take the damaged or stolen (if recovered) property after paying for it so that the insured can not have the payment and the property at the same time. If the insured were to be guaranteed the insurance payment and the property, this would amount to unjust enrichment for the insured and this is not the purpose of insurance.

The current version of the BAP also has a provision here that if the insurer pays for the loss, the payment will include the applicable sales tax for the damaged or stolen property. Some have questioned whether payment for a loss to a covered auto should include sales taxes, an item that cannot be valued or depreciated based on its physical condition. This part of the loss condition should clarify the issue.

Transfer of the Rights of Recovery

The fifth loss condition deals with subrogation. The title of the condition is "transfer of rights of recovery against others to us." The insurer declares that if any person or organization to or for whom the insurer makes payment under the BAP has rights to recover damages from another, those rights are transferred to the insurer. Like other parts of the BAP, this condition works to keep the insured (or some other party) from unjust enrichment. For example, if the insured's auto has been negligently damaged by another party and the insured collects physical damage coverage from his or her own insurer, this loss condition attempts to prevent the insured from also collecting a property damage liability payment from the other party; the insured has been made whole by his or her own insurer and it would be unfair to allow the insured to collect a second payment for the same damage. The insurer has expended money for the physical damage to the covered auto, and it has a right to be reimbursed for that expenditure from the negligent party.

This loss condition also requires the person or organization to or for whom payment has been made to help the insurer secure the right of recovery. The condition notes that the person or organization must do nothing after the accident or loss to impair the recovery rights. Therefore, if the insured has, for example, made a hold harmless agreement with a customer before an accident happens that damages the covered auto, this condition will not void that agreement. The insured had agreed before the loss not to hold the customer liable for any damage to the covered auto and the insurer is bound by this pre-loss agreement. It can not subrogate against the customer for any physical damage payment made to repair the auto.

General Conditions

The business auto form has eight general conditions.

Bankruptcy

The bankruptcy condition simply states that the insurer will not be relieved of any obligation under the BAP if the insured becomes bankrupt or insolvent.

Concealment, Misrepresentation, or Fraud

The concealment, misrepresentation, or fraud condition makes the coverage form void in any case of fraud by the named insured at any time as that fraud relates to the coverage form. If the condition stopped there, that would mean that only fraud by the named insured could void the policy. However, the condition goes on to state that the BAP is void if the named insured or any other insured at any time intentionally conceals or misrepresents a material fact concerning the coverage form, the covered auto, the named insured's interest in the covered auto, or a claim under the BAP.

For example, if the named insured's employee was involved in an accident while driving a covered auto and then lied about the facts of the accident, this condition voids the policy. The named insured is put into a serious situation because of the actions of another, but the fight against insurance fraud requires tough measures. Of course, if the insurer is claiming the policy is void due to fraud, it must prove the fraud exists; it must prove an insured intentionally concealed or misrepresented a material fact. The burden of proof is on the insurer.

Liberalization

The third general condition is the liberalization clause. The insurer tells the insured here that if it revises the business auto coverage form without an additional premium charge, the policy will automatically provide the additional coverage as of the day the revision is effective in the named insured's state. For example, if the insurer revises an exclusion in a way that additional coverage is provided to the insured, and this revision is made with no premium charge, the coverage is provided to the insured the same day that the change becomes effective in the state of the named insured; no endorsements or notices are necessary for the insured to have the coverage.

The only question is when the change is effective in the state of the named insured. Some states have a file and use system; some have a use and file system; some require prior approval before the policies or changes can be used. The insured is not expected to know this information, so it is up to the insured's agent or broker to keep the insured informed on the subject.

No Benefit to Bailee

The fourth general condition deals with bailee benefits; there are none under the BAP. The condition states that the insurer will not recognize any assignment or grant any physical damage coverage for the benefit of any person or organization holding, storing, or transporting property for a fee. The insurer is declaring, for example, that if the insured has its covered autos stored at another entity's parking lot and the cars are damaged, the parking lot owner can not look to the insured's BAP for coverage. The BAP was written to cover damage to the insured's autos and not to provide coverage for another entity that is liable for damaging those autos. If the insured's covered autos are damaged while in storage, the physical damage coverage of the BAP will pay for the damage, but the bailee benefits clause makes sure that the parking facility owner will, if liable, reimburse the insurer for the payments. The bailee is to receive no benefits, direct or indirect, under the insured's auto policy.

Other Insurance

The other insurance clause is the fifth general condition. It declares that coverage for covered autos owned by the named insured is primary and that coverage for covered autos not owned by the named insured is excess over any other collectible insurance. As for trailers, if the trailer is connected to a nonowned vehicle, the liability coverage is excess; if the trailer is connected to a covered owned by the named insured, the liability coverage is primary.

Hired auto physical damage coverage is treated differently. Any covered auto that the named insured leases, hires, rents or borrows is deemed to be a covered auto owned by the named insured and so, has primary coverage under the BAP for physical damage. For example, if the named insured rents a car for its CEO to use while on a business trip and the BAP has hired auto physical damage coverage, and that car is damaged while the CEO is using it, the named insured's BAP will treat the rental as an owned car and pay for the physical damage on a primary basis.

The BAP's liability coverage is primary for any liability assumed under an insured contract. The definition of "insured contract" is discussed later, but basically, the insured has assumed the liability of another and the insurer has agreed to this; it would be contradictory for the insurer to agree to cover this assumption of liability and then say such coverage is excess over the other party's insurance.

Finally, this condition sets the tone for shared coverage. If the BAP and any other coverage form covers on the same basis, the sharing of the coverage is proportional to the total of the limits of all the coverage forms. So, if the insured's BAP has BI liability limits of $50,000 and another policy has BI limits of $250,000 and a third policy has BI limits of $500,000, the total of these limits is $800,000; if there is a loss and all the policies have to pay, the insured's BAP will pay 1/16th ($50,000 divided by $800,000) of the claim's total.

Premium Audit

The premium audit clause states that the premium charged at the beginning of the policy period is an estimated one, based on the existing exposures as related to the insurer by the named insured. Because such exposures can change during the policy period, this clause enables the insurer to determine the actual exposures that have existed during the policy period through an audit and then charge the appropriate premium. If the final premium is more than the estimated initial premium, the first named insured gets the bill; if the final premium is less than the initial premium, the first named insured gets the refund.

The due date for the final premium or retrospective premium is the date shown as the due date on the bill sent to the first named insured. This point is in response to an accounting guideline issued by the National Association of Insurance Commissioners (NAIC) that stated that if the due date for audit premiums is not addressed in an insurance policy, any uncollected audit premium will be considered nonadmitted on an insurer's statement.

Policy Period/Coverage Territory

The next general condition describes the policy period and the coverage territory. The policy period is stated on the declarations form and the coverage under the policy is for losses and accidents that occur during the stated period. The coverage territory is the United States (including territories and possessions), Puerto Rico, and Canada. Mexico is not part of the coverage territory and any insured planning on operating an auto in Mexico needs to be aware of that fact.

The BAP does offer an extension of the coverage territory. The policy will cover loss to or accidents involving a covered auto while being transported between any of the places listed as "the coverage territory". For example, if the insured is having its covered auto shipped from North Carolina to Puerto Rico and a fire on the ship destroys the car while en route in the Atlantic Ocean, the BAP will pay for the loss to that auto. Of course, the insured needs to have chosen the appropriate physical damage coverage in case of such a loss to the car. If the insured had purchased only collision coverage, damage by fire would not be covered even if the loss occurred within the coverage territory.

Another extension of the coverage territory may, at first, seem quite extensive. A part of the coverage territory definition on the current BAP states that the coverage territory is "anywhere in the world". However, this extension is dependent on certain requirements. One of these is that the insured leases, hires, rents, or borrows a private passenger type car (without a driver) for a period of thirty days or less. Another requirement is that the insured's responsibility to pay damages is determined in a lawsuit on the merits in the United States of America, Puerto Rico, or Canada. As an example: the insured goes to England for a two week vacation and rents a car to drive around the countryside. While doing this, the insured accidentally crashes into an oncoming vehicle and severely injures the other driver. The insured is then sued in a court in his home state of Ohio over the damages. If the Ohio court finds the insured responsible for the damages, the insured's BAP will apply to the loss.

The BAP's worldwide coverage is not automatic, but it does offer the insured a sense of comfort while driving in countries other than the U.S. or Canada. Of course, the insured should be aware of the provisions of the Other Insurance clause on the BAP and the effect that that clause may have on his worldwide coverage. This is because some countries (for example, Mexico) may require or strongly advise the insured to buy insurance from a domestic insurer rather than relying on the driver's own stateside policy. And, the credit card used by the insured to rent his car may provide some coverage. So, if the insured does have other collectible insurance on his rented car, his BAP liability coverage is on an excess basis, in most cases.

Two or More Coverage Forms

The last general condition discusses what happens when two or more coverage forms issued by the insurer to the named insured apply to the same accident as primary insurance. The aggregate maximum limit of insurance under all the coverage forms shall not exceed the highest applicable limit of insurance under any one coverage form. In other words, the insurer is trying to prevent stacking of limits of multiple policies it has issued to the named insured. For example, if the insured has three auto policies from ABC Insurance Company covering liability claims in the amounts of $50,000, $150,000, and $250,000, and an accident occurs that involves all three policies, the most the insurer will pay is $250,000. The question of whether to allow stacking is subject to state law and court decisions, but this clause enables the insurer to, at the very least, declare that the insurance contract forbids stacking and the insured has signed on to that provision.

Common Policy Conditions

IL 00 17, common policy conditions, is a form that must be attached to the BAP as it is to all policies written under ISO's commercial insurance program. IL 00 17 contains six conditions that affect the BAP: cancellation, changes, examination of books and records, inspections and surveys, premiums, and transfer of rights and duties under the policy.

Cancellation

The cancellation condition notes that the first named insured may cancel the policy by mailing or delivering to the insurer advance written notice of cancellation. The first named insured can send the policy back to the insurer or write a letter requesting cancellation at any time during the policy period. If the insured requests the cancellation, any refund of premium may be less than on a pro rata basis. The insurer has a right to certain expenses and costs involved in issuing and then cancelling a policy; if the insured is the one requesting the cancellation, he or she should expect that any refund will reflect the expenses and costs that the insurer has incurred.

If the insurer wants the policy cancelled, it has to mail or deliver to the first named insured written notice of cancellation. If the cancellation is due to the nonpayment of premium, the insurer has to give the insured at least the (10) days notice before the effective date of the cancellation. If the cancellation is for any other reason, the notice period is thirty (30) days. Any refund is on a pro rata basis since the insurer is the one seeking cancellation. Cancellation of an insurance policy is also subject to state law, which can vary from state to state. For information on the various cancellation laws, see National Underwriter's annual *Cancellation and NonRenewal Handbook*.

Changes

The changes condition states that all the agreements between the named insured and the insurer concerning the afforded insurance is contained in the policy. There can be no side agreements or "understandings" between the insured and his or her agent that modify the policy provisions. The terms of the policy can be amended or waived only by endorsement issued by the insurer. The first named insured is authorized to make changes in the terms of the policy but only with the consent of the insurer.

Examination of Books

The third condition on IL 00 17 states that the insurer may examine and audit the named insured's books and records as they relate to the policy at any time during the policy period and up to three years afterward. The insurer has the right to know what exposures it has when writing an auto policy for the insured. The insurer also has the right to charge an appropriate premium for the exposures it covers. One way for the insurer to become aware of the exposures is through an examination of the insured's books and records and this clause gives the insurer the right to do so. However, this right does not mean that the insurer has been given carte blanche to examine any and all records belonging to the insured; the records must relate to the insurance policy. Furthermore, this right of examination is limited to the books and records of the named insured, not every insured under the policy.

Inspections and Surveys

The fourth condition gives the insurer the right, but not the obligation, to make inspections and surveys at any time. The insurer also can give the named insured reports on the conditions found and recommend changes. Some courts had looked at this condition and declared that it placed the insurer in the position of a self-declared safety inspector which, in turn, made the insurer ultimately responsible for any subsequent loss or accident. In answer to this, the condition goes on to declare that any inspections, surveys, reports or recommendations relate only to insurability and the premiums to be charged. The insurer does not make safety inspections. Besides, as noted, the insurer can only make recommendations; the ultimate responsibility for any changes to improve the exposures lies with the insured.

Premiums

The fifth condition makes the first named insured shown in the declarations the responsible party for payment of all premiums and the payee for any returned premiums. This simplifies the process, but leaves any other insureds at the mercy of the first named insured. For example, should the first named insured fail to make the premium payments with the result that the policy is cancelled, the other insureds would be uninsured and not even know it.

Transfer of Rights and Duties

The last common policy condition deals with the transfer of rights and duties under the policy. The named insured's rights and duties may not be transferred without the written consent of the insurer, except in the case of death of an individual named insured. This clause is an anti-assignment clause in that the insurer does not want the insured to transfer its rights or duties to some other party without the insurer knowing about it. This condition protects the insurer from unknown and unwanted exposures.

6

Business Auto Definitions

The business auto coverage form has 16 definitions.

"Accident"

The term "accident" leads off the definitions section of the policy. The wording of the definition does not really explain what an accident is; it merely says that an accident includes continuous or repeated exposure to the same conditions resulting in bodily injury or property damage. Therefore, any question about what an accident is will have to defer to the every day commonly used dictionary meaning. *Merriam Webster's Collegiate Dictionary, Tenth Edition,* states that an accident is "an unforeseen and unplanned event; something happening by chance rather than by design."

Liability coverage under the BAP is based on BI or PD caused by an accident and the physical damage coverage is for direct and accidental loss. The first exclusion under the liability coverage section of the BAP applies to BI or PD expected or intended from the standpoint of the insured. So the point is, the insurance policy is meant to apply to events that are unforeseen and unplanned—an accident.

"Auto"

The second definition is "auto." An auto is a land motor vehicle, trailer, or semitrailer designed for travel on public roads, but does not include mobile equipment. There are two important points here.

First, since an auto is a land motor vehicle, that would extend the scope of the definition to include things like mopeds, motorcycles, three-wheelers, motor homes, and trucks; all these things are designed for travel on public roads. It may not be the intention of the insurer to have the business auto policy apply to mopeds or three-wheelers or motor homes, but the definition of "auto" would allow that to happen; proper underwriting of a risk before policy inception would be a safeguard for the intentions of the insurer.

Second, the definition of auto specifically declares that an auto does not include mobile equipment. Liability for the ownership or use of mobile equipment is handled through the general liability coverage form, so the BAP wants to draw a clear distinction between an auto and mobile equipment. Sometimes the lines of distinction may blur. (Note that endorsement CA 00 51 is an endorsement meant to further clarify the distinction between an auto and mobile equipment; see Chapter 11 for more information on this endorsement.)

Is the Vehicle Considered Mobile Equipment or an Auto?

The insured owns a four-wheel all-terrain vehicle (ATV) which is used in his business and for pleasure. He owns a large tract of land and has his land manager patrol the area with the vehicle and occasionally uses the vehicle to go hunting. The insured could take the ATV onto public roads, but maintains that he does not and wants to use the ATV only on his land. The issue is whether the insured's CGL form would apply to the use of the ATV or whether the auto policy is more proper.

It is true that an auto is defined as a land motor vehicle designed for travel on public roads, and the ATV can fit that description. However, part of the definition of mobile equipment includes vehicles maintained for use solely on or next to premises owned by the named insured. And, the definition of auto states that it does not include mobile equipment. This should be interpreted to mean that if a vehicle happens to fit the definitions of both an auto and mobile equipment, it must fall into the mobile equipment category. The intention of the insured is to use the ATV as mobile equipment (for use on his land only), and that, backed up by the definitions of auto and mobile equipment, make the CGL form the proper policy for the ATV's liability coverage.

"Bodily Injury"

The BAP declares that bodily injury means bodily injury, sickness or disease, including death resulting from any of these. The issue of whether mental injury or emotional injury equals bodily injury may arise in a claim, but most courts today require some actual physical injury to the body before a BI claim can be established.

"Covered Pollution Cost or Expense"

The liability insuring agreement under the BAP includes coverage for a covered pollution cost or expense—this is a defined term. The term means any cost or expense arising out of any request, demand, order, or statutory or regulatory requirement, or any claim or suit by or on behalf of a governmental authority demanding that the insured or others test for, monitor, clean up or in any way respond to or assess the effects of pollutants—basically, clean up costs. However, even though the BAP offers this coverage, the coverage is not unlimited. The limitations on coverage can be found in the insuring agreement and in the definition of covered pollution cost or expense itself.

The insuring agreement states that a covered pollution cost or expense will be paid only if there is BI or PD to which the BAP applies that is caused by the same accident that caused the pollution cost or expense. The definition states that a covered pollution cost or expense does not include costs or expenses arising out of spills of pollutants that are being transported in a covered auto or otherwise in the course of transit by the insured. And, a covered pollution cost or expense does not include a spill of pollutants before the pollutants are moved into a covered auto, or after the pollutants are moved from the covered auto.

To make things more convoluted, there are exceptions to these limitations. Namely, if the pollutants happen to be the fuels, lubricants, and fluids needed for the normal mechanical functioning of the covered auto (such as, gasoline or oil), and these pollutants leak from the gas tank or auto part designed by the manufacturer to hold them, the clean up costs will be deemed to be a covered pollution cost or expense. And, if the covered auto knocks over a storage tank on the property of someone other than an insured and a pollutant spills out, this is also considered a covered pollution cost or expense. Chapter Three of this book—Liability Coverage—offers some examples of the exceptions and the circumstances under which the BAP would pay for a covered pollution cost or expense.

That part of the definition pertaining to a statutory or regulatory requirement demanding the insured clean up the effects of pollutants makes the point that there is no requirement that someone demand or request the insured to act to clean up a pollution discharge. The definition requires merely that a law or regulation be in the legal code for the policy provisions to come into play. As an example, there may be some statute or regulation on the books that would require the insured to clean up a pollution spill, but for whatever reason, no entity has taken the initiative to demand action on the part of the insured. Now, the fact that no one has forced the insured into action will not remove the insured's responsibility for the clean up because the existence of a statute or regulation dictating a clean up will make the insured responsible for the clean up. And, if that is the case, the covered pollution cost or expense insuring agreement will apply. This part of the definition enables the insured to have coverage without the insurer's being able to deny coverage because there was no one requesting or demanding or ordering a clean up.

"Diminution in Value"

Diminution in value means the actual or perceived loss in market value or resale value that results from a direct and accidental loss. This definition helps to understand the scope of the diminution in value exclusion that is in the physical damage coverage section of the BAP. The physical damage coverage is for actual physical damage (direct) to the covered auto, and an indirect loss such as a loss in market value or resale value is not meant to be covered under the terms of the BAP.

"Employee"

The sixth definition on the BAP is "employee." The BAP does not define an employee as a dictionary might; it merely states that an employee includes a leased worker, but not a temporary worker. The terms, leased employee and temporary worker, are also defined on the BAP and will be discussed later. The important thing to remember about the definition of "employee" is that leased employees are considered the same as regular employees when it comes to coverages, exclusions, and conditions under the BAP.

"Insured"

The term "insured" is the seventh definition. An "insured" is defined as any person or organization qualifying as an insured in the Who Is An Insured provision of the liability coverage section of the BAP (see Chapter 3). This definition also includes the severability or separation of insureds information in that the coverage is said to be applied separately to each insured seeking coverage or against whom a claim or suit is brought.

The "separation of insureds" phrase means that each insured has to be looked at individually when it comes to the coverages, exclusions, and conditions of the BAP. For example, liability exclusion number one— expected or intended injury—precludes coverage for BI or PD expected or intended from the standpoint of the insured. If there is only one insured involved in the event, this wording is uncomplicated. However, if there are two or more insureds involved, does the fact that the exclusion applies to one mean it applies to all?

> ### The Separation of Insureds
>
> *An employee of the named insured was driving the named insured's auto on company business when he caught sight of a neighbor with whom he was feuding driving down the street. The employee chased the neighbor for three blocks and deliberately crashed the named insured's auto into the neighbor's car, injuring the neighbor and demolishing the neighbor's car. The neighbor sued the employee and the named insured; the insurer declined coverage due to the expected or intended injury clause. The named insured expects coverage since there was no intent to injure on its part.*
>
> The exclusion applies only to the insured that expected or intended the injury. The exclusion is worded so as to apply to "the" insured and this wording limits the scope of the exclusion. If the word "an" had been used, then the case can be made that if the exclusion applies to one insured (an insured), it applies to all insureds. However, "the" insured is specific and applies individually and separately. The separation of insureds clause in the policy states that the coverage applies separately to each insured, so the exclusion of the coverage has to apply separately also.

There are other instances on the BAP where the separation of insureds should be noted. For example, the care, custody, or control exclusion talks about "the insured's" care, custody or control. Another exclusion specifically applies to the named insured, that is, "your work"—the completed operations exclusion. And, the duties in the event of an accident clause notes that "you and any other involved insured" have to perform certain tasks. The bottom line is that if there is any confusion on the part of an insured as to whether he or she has coverage under the BAP, or whether he or she has certain duties to perform, the agent or broker must be aware of the separation of insureds principle and inform the insureds accordingly.

"Insured Contract"

"Insured contract" is the next defined term. The definition is similar to the one found on the CGL form, including the lease of premises, sidetrack agreements, easement agreements, and the obligation to indemnify a municipality parts. Whether these parts of the definition have much relevance to business auto coverage is debatable. However, other parts of the definition do have a more obvious impact on business auto coverage.

An insured contract also includes that part of any contract or agreement pertaining to the business of the named insured under which the named insured assumes the tort liability of another to pay for BI or PD to a third party or organization. For example, the named insured is delivering items for customers, and, as part of the business contract between the named insured and the customer, the named insured has agreed to save and hold harmless the customer against liability in connection with the deliveries; a third party is injured while the named insured is delivering the customer's goods; the injured party sues the named insured and the customer; since the named insured has agreed to assume the tort liability of the customer, the ultimate obligation to pay any judgment or settlement falls upon the named insured. The insured contract definition gives the named insured liability coverage for that obligation.

Note that this contractual liability insurance is concerned only with tort liability assumed by the named insured. Contractual liability insurance under the BAP has no applicability to liability resulting from a breach of contract.

Another part of the insured contract definition deals with that part of any contract or agreement entered into, as part of the named insured's business, that pertains to the rental or lease of any auto by the named insured or any employee. Coverage under this provision is guided by the specific terms of the car rental contract, but if, for example, the rental contract calls for the named insured to assume the liability of the car rental firm for any accidents that arise from the use of the rented car, this section of the insured contract definition will apply.

Even though the insured has coverage for responsibilities agreed to under the terms of the rental contract, he or she needs to read the rental contract carefully to be aware of the responsibilities that have been accepted. One of the main reasons for this is that an "insured contract" does not extend to include paying for property damage to any auto rented or leased by the named insured or employees. Even if the rental contract requires the named insured to pay for damage done to the rented car, the BAP does not consider this as part of an "insured contract;" liability coverage will not apply. Of course, the damage done to the car can be covered under the physical damage section of the BAP if the insured has symbol 1 or symbol 8 on the dec page next to the physical damage coverages, but such coverage is not part of the insured contract section.

Another point to consider is that an insured contract does not include a car rental contract that calls for an auto loaned, leased, or rented to be accompanied by a driver. If the car rental comes with a driver, the BAP will not consider the rental contract to be an insured contract. The insurer would prefer to have the named insured or his or her employees drive covered autos so as to have some control over the exposures; rented drivers present an unknown exposure to the insurer and are discouraged.

An insured contract also does not include that part of any contract or agreement that indemnifies a railroad for bodily injury or property damage arising out of construction or demolition operations within fifty (50) feet of any railroad property. The BAP is not meant to apply to liability arising out of the insured's assuming the liability of a railroad through a hold harmless agreement—there are other liability forms for this purpose.

"Leased Worker"

If the insured wants to lease workers (even drivers), that is acceptable to the insurer. Leased workers are treated as regular employees under the provisions of the BAP; however, the leased worker has to meet the terms of the definition. A "leased worker" is a person leased to the named insured by a labor leasing firm under an agreement to perform duties related to the conduct of the named insured's business. This obviously does not include a car rental company since it is in the business of renting cars and not leasing laborers. However, if the named insured contracts with a labor leasing firm for a worker, that worker will be considered an employee of the named insured while doing the business of the named insured, even if that business is driving a rented car.

"Loss"

The business auto policy defines "loss" since that is part of the insuring agreement under the physical damage section. A "loss" is direct and accidental loss or damage. Of course, damage to a covered auto should be accidental. Auto physical damage coverage is not meant to apply to damage deliberately caused by the insured; that is not the purpose of insurance.

The key word in the definition of loss is "direct." By the use of the word "direct," the insurer is saying that a physical damage loss is different from a property damage loss in that property damage includes loss of use (which is an indirect loss), but a physical damage loss does not. The insured needs to be aware of this distinction, especially if a hired or nonowned auto is involved.

Is Loss of Use a Covered Loss?

The insured rented an auto for use on company business and had symbol 8—hired autos—on his business auto policy. An accident occurred for which the insured was liable. The auto policy paid for the physical damage to the rented auto, but didn't pay for the loss of use claim. If this was a covered auto, why wasn't the loss of use claim paid?

(scenario continues next page)

> *(scenario continues next page)*
>
> The use of symbol 8 on the BAP will provide coverage for hired, rented, or borrowed autos. However, the coverage does have its limits. Symbol 8 will give the insured liability coverage for BI or PD, but the care, custody, or control exclusion removes property damage coverage for property in the insured's care, custody, or control. As for the physical damage coverage, the BAP would pay for damage to the rented car, but the coverage is for direct loss; loss of use is not a direct loss, but rather a consequence of the direct loss. A loss under the physical damage part of the BAP is actual physical damage to the auto itself; consequences of that actual damage are not included in the definition of "loss" on the BAP.
>
> One possible way for the loss of use to be covered is to sidestep the care, custody, or control exclusion. This could be done by use of a manuscripted endorsement, if the insurer is willing. Or, the exclusion can be read very narrowly so that "the insured" refers only to the driver of the rented car at the time of the accident. For example, if the named insured is a company and its employee is driving the rented auto at the time of the accident, both the company and the employee are insureds under the BAP. However, a case can be made that the auto was not in the care or control of the named insured, only in the care of the employee. There would be no PD liability coverage for the employee due to the care, custody, or control exclusion; but, since the named insured did not have custody or control of the rented car, the exclusion should not apply. The use of the word "the" limits the scope of the exclusion in its applicability to insureds. "The" insured who had care, custody, or control of the rented car was the employee and not the named insured.

"Mobile Equipment"

The definition of "mobile equipment" in the BAP tries to make a clear distinction between an auto and mobile equipment. The definition of mobile equipment is detailed and is weighted heavily in favor of vehicles not usually used on public roads. Examples include bulldozers, farm machinery, vehicles that travel on crawler treads, vehicles that provide mobility to power cranes, shovels, road construction equipment, and vehicles maintained primarily for purposes other than the transportation of persons or cargo. This is not to say that mobile equipment can never travel on public roads, but that the primary use—and the primary exposure to a loss—is off public roadways. The business auto policy is for risks with the main exposure being driving in public, using the public roads. The business auto policy is for autos, and the auto definition along with the detailed definition of mobile equipment on the BAP are meant to help insureds and insurers know when the BAP applies.

"Pollutants"

"Pollutants" are defined as any solid, liquid, gaseous or thermal irritant or contaminant. Obviously, this is a very general definition and problems have arisen when insurers try to use the definition to include any type of substance in order to deny a claim; for example, a bottle of ink spilled on a carpet or a motor oil spilled into a car radiator. Some courts are limiting the definition to environmental contaminants as opposed to any substance that could fit the dictionary definition of "contaminant." The issue is not close to being a settled one.

"Property Damage"

"Property damage" is damage to or loss of use of tangible property; this definition has to be seen in contrast to the definition of "loss," as described previously. "Property damage" is used in connection with the insured's liability to others and that is why loss of use is included in the definition. So for example, if the insured is liable for damaging a delivery van, the property damage liability coverage would apply not only to the direct damage to the van, but also to the amount of income lost by the injured party arising out of loss of use of the van. Since the insured is responsible for the van not being used, it is only fair and right that the responsibility extend to the income lost by not being able to use the van.

"Suit"

The term "suit" is defined as a civil proceeding in which damages because of bodily injury or property damage or a covered pollution cost or expense to which the BAP applies are alleged. "Suit" includes an arbitration proceeding or any other alternative dispute resolution proceeding. The insurer has agreed to defend any insured against "suits" and this definition makes the point that insured will be defended by the insurer in alternative dispute resolution proceedings and not just lawsuits.

"Temporary Worker"

The BAP defines "temporary worker." That person is one who is furnished to the named insured to substitute for a permanent employee on leave or to meet seasonal or short-term workload conditions. This means several things.

First, the temporary worker is not considered a regular employee—he substitutes for a permanent employee. Therefore, if a temporary worker is injured due to the negligence of the named insured, the auto policy will respond to a claim against the named insured because the workers compensation and employers liability exclusions do not apply.

The temporary worker is furnished to the named insured, implying that some outside entity may have contracted with the named insured to furnish the temp. There are contractual implications for the named insured to consider in this situation, and one of them is that an insured contract does not include a contract that pertains to the loan, lease, or rental of an auto if it comes with a driver. So, if the temp comes furnished with a car to be used on the insured's business, contractual liability coverage through an insured contract does not exist.

Finally, the temp is furnished only for certain work situations, that is, while permanent employees are on leave or to meet seasonal or short-term workload conditions. This implies that there is a finite time period for the temporary worker's employment; there is to be no long-term employment relationship established between the named insured employer and the temporary worker. As an example, the named insured florist who, at Easter or Mothers Day, hires college students to handle the seasonal increase in flower deliveries. The students are working for the named insured for a finite time period, usually one week or less, and they are there just to supplement the regular workforce of the named insured due to the holiday work overload; no permanent employment is the contemplated goal of the insured or the temp.

One more point. The distinctive description of the temporary worker—as well as that of the leased worker—tries to ensure that the two types of workers are not confused. And, it is important not to confuse them because leased workers are considered employees of the named insured while temporary workers are not. Both can be insureds under the terms of the BAP, but only leased workers are considered employees of the named insured. And, as noted previously, the fact that temporary workers are not considered employees of the named insured has relevance. For example, if a temp is driving a covered auto on the business of the named insured and causes an accident, the named insured will be covered for a claim since he or she is an insured for any covered auto. The temp is an insured if he or she is using a covered auto with the permission of the named insured. However, since the temp is not considered an employee of the named insured, he or she can file a claim against the named insured for any injuries suffered and no "employee" exclusion will apply.

"Trailer"

The last definition in the BAP is "trailer." The definition simply declares that a trailer includes semitrailers. Since both trailers and semitrailers are considered autos on the BAP, this particular definition may seem superfluous. However, the BAP does talk about "autos" separately from "trailers" throughout the body of the policy, so a separate definition may help clarify coverage questions should they arise.

7

Auto Medical Payments Coverage

Auto medical payments coverage for the business auto policy is available through the addition of endorsement CA 99 03. The concept of medical payments coverage under the BAP is the same as that under other insurance forms, namely, to offer payment for medical services needed because of an accident, without requiring liability on the part of the insured.

In many instances, the insured purchases med pay coverage for "goodwill" purposes so that, for example, if a customer is injured in an accident involving the insured, the insured can get the medical services paid quickly and keep the customer happy. There is also a sound legal basis for having med pay coverage quickly take care of an accident victim's medical expenses—if an injured person is cared for immediately and his expenses paid, it may forestall future lawsuits against the insured based on those injuries (while it is true that med pay is not based on the insured's legal liability, the insured could still be sued for injuries suffered by another and this entails, at the very least, defense costs); so, med pay coverage really earns its designation as "insurance."

As noted previously, CA 99 03 is the endorsement by which medical payments coverage can be added to a BAP. This chapter offers a discussion of that endorsement.

Coverage

Endorsement CA 99 03 declares that the insurer will pay reasonable expenses incurred for necessary medical and funeral services to or for an insured who sustains bodily injury caused by an accident. Only those expenses incurred for services rendered within three years of the date of the accident will be paid.

The first item that deserves comment is the term "reasonable expenses." Just what are reasonable expenses? This can be a relative, subjective term, depending mightily on whether you are the injured person or the insurer. However, with managed care the vogue these days, most insurers have solid information and statistics available to them to use as guidelines for what medical expenses should be for particular injuries. For example, it can be charted that in a certain locality, a broken arm might cost $100 to set at an area hospital; if the bill presented to the insurer is for $600, the insurer may very well wonder why and dispute the cost. In any case though, the very vagueness of the phrase "reasonable expenses" should allow for open discussion and compromise between the insured and the insurer.

Med pay coverage is for the expenses incurred by an insured who sustains bodily injury caused by an accident. "Insured" is a defined term on the endorsement and will be discussed later. "Bodily injury" and "accident" mean the same here as in the business auto policy which CA 99 03 modifies.

What are the "Expenses Incurred"?

The insured was covered under a business auto policy that included auto medical payments coverage with a limit of $5,000. A one-vehicle accident occurred in which the insured was killed. The insured's family submitted the bill from the funeral home to the insurer in the amount of $4,800. The invoice indicated that the insured had purchased a burial policy in the amount of $4,000; this left a balance due of $800. The insurer is stating that it is only obligated to pay the $800 as the med pay endorsement declares "we will pay only those expenses incurred ...." The family believes that the entire $4,800 should be paid. Which view should prevail?

The insurer is not correct in its interpretation of med pay coverage. The insuring agreement on the med pay endorsement states that the insurer will pay for reasonable expenses incurred for necessary medical and funeral services; it does not state that these expenses are covered unless some other insurance or payment plan applies. The insured paid a premium for the medical payments coverage and there is no exclusion or limitation that would apply in this instance.

Besides, the med pay endorsement has a clause that declares that the reference to other insurance on the BAP applies only to other collectible auto medical payments insurance. And, the limit of insurance clause on the endorsement indicates that no duplicate payments will be paid under the med pay coverage and any liability coverage form, uninsured motorists coverage form, or any underinsured motorists coverage form; there is not one word about burial policies. If the insurer had wanted to limit the amount payable to the insured based on other payments such as a burial policy or a pre-paid funeral arrangement, it should have specifically included that information in the med pay endorsement.

Another term to consider is the phrase "expenses incurred, for services rendered within three years from the date of the accident." This is the insurer telling the insured that the medical (or funeral) services have to be rendered, that is, actually given, in order for the insurer to pay the bill. In addition, the services must be rendered within the specified three-year time period. This requirement could conflict with the accident victim's doctor's medical opinion which could lead to some coverage disputes.

> ### When Must Services Be Rendered To Be Covered Under Med Pay?
>
> *A young insured sustained injury to his mouth and gums in an auto accident. Due to the insured's age, the oral surgeon suggested that final repairs be deferred until the boy was considerably older. The policy (and the insurer) stated that the services must be rendered within three years of the accident in order for any medical payments to be paid under the med pay endorsement. The insured's parents believe that the insurer is not being realistic and is ignoring valid medical advice. Doesn't the oral surgeon's medical opinion carry any weight in this issue?*
>
> The insuring agreement on the med pay endorsement takes precedence. The expenses incurred have to be for services rendered within three years of the date of the accident. Setting time limits for coverage under an insurance policy is acceptable and based on sound actuarial practices. While it is true that ignoring the doctor's medical advice sounds unreasonable, the three year time limit is valid if the insurer wants to strictly adhere to the contract.

Who Is An Insured?

There are three classes of insureds under the terms of CA 99 03. The named insured, of course, is an insured while occupying any auto, or, if a pedestrian, when struck by any auto. If the named insured is an individual, any family member while occupying or, if a pedestrian, when struck by any auto. Finally, anyone else occupying a covered auto or a temporary substitute for a covered auto is also an insured. Note that the temporary substitute, while not defined on CA 99 03, is meant to be an auto that has taken the place of a covered auto that is temporarily out of service because of its breakdown, repair, servicing, loss, or destruction.

There would be nothing really out of the ordinary in these descriptions of insureds, except for the fact that a business auto policy often has a corporation or a partnership as a named insured. Clearly, a corporation or a partnership can not occupy a car or walk down the sidewalk; so, the first category of insureds would have relevance only if the named insured is an individual.

The second category recognizes this point, in that it specifically mentions the named insured as an individual. This is reinforced by the policy definition of "family member" as a person related to the named insured by blood, marriage, or adoption who is also a resident of the named insured's household. Obviously, an individual can have family members, but a corporation or a partnership can not.

The last category is very broad in scope. *Anyone* occupying a covered auto is an insured. Since "anyone" is such a general term, any limitation on who is an insured in this category must arise from the "occupying" or "covered auto" portions of the definition, or from exclusions that are on CA 99 03 (for example, the employee exclusion). Whether or not an auto is a covered auto is, of course, dependent on the designation symbol shown on the declarations page. "Occupying" is defined on CA 99 03 as "in, upon, getting in, on, out or off". So, anyone who fits this definition is an insured under med pay coverage.

The limitation on the scope of who is an insured in the first two categories may be a major reason why commercial insureds do not purchase auto med pay coverage as commonly as personal auto insureds. The coverage offered by CA 99 03 probably seems unnecessary to a corporate insured. On the other hand, if the named insured is an individual or a company that routinely carries passengers in its automobiles or allows customers to drive its autos (for example, taxi or bus companies, car dealers, car rental firms), buying auto med pay coverage certainly makes good business sense.

Exclusions

Endorsement CA 99 03 has eight exclusions.

Medical payments insurance does not apply to bodily injury sustained by an insured while occupying a vehicle located for use as a premises. If an insured is going to make a vehicle his or her premises, a homeowners policy or some kind of dwelling policy is the proper way to insure medical payments coverage. This exclusion takes auto insurance out of this equation.

Med pay also does not apply to bodily injury to the named insured while occupying or struck by any vehicle, other than a covered auto, owned by the named insured or furnished for the named insured's regular use. The same is true of bodily injury to family members. This is simply an attempt by the insurer to make sure that the insured's autos are covered under the business auto policy. This controls the risk exposures, and provides the proper premium for the insured's declared exposures.

The next exclusion applies to bodily injury to the named insured's employees arising out of and in the course of employment by the named insured. If the employees are injured during the course of their employment, workers compensation is the way to cover the injuries. The exclusion emphasizes this idea in that it goes on to state that bodily injury to domestic employees *not entitled to workers compensation benefits* is covered. Note that state law concerning workers comp coverage for domestic employees differs according to the individual state. Some states require workers comp for domestics, some make it voluntary, some specifically exclude domestics from the workers comp law. Even in those states where workers comp is required for domestics, coverage can be based on the amount earned or the hours worked or a combination of the two. The insured's agent or broker should be familiar with state law in this regard so as to advise the insured if med pay is available to domestic employees.

The endorsement (CA 99 03) defines a domestic employee as a person engaged in household or domestic work performed principally in connection with a residence premises. If the named insured is a corporation, partnership, or limited liability company (LLC), it is difficult to see the applicability of this domestic employee discussion. However, since the named insured could be an individual, CA 99 03 wants to give med pay to domestic employees of the named insured just in case one of their duties involves driving a covered auto. For example, if the named insured is John Doe and he has his maid drive a covered auto to the store to pick up a package and the maid is not covered by workers comp statutes, CA 99 03 allows medical payments to the maid if she is injured in an auto accident.

CA 99 03 does not apply to bodily injury to an insured while working in a business that sells, services, repairs or parks autos unless that business is owned by the named insured. The definition of an insured under CA 99 03 includes anyone occupying a covered auto. So, for example, a parking lot attendant could be considered an insured any time he or she parks the named insured's covered auto, and thus receive medical payments for an injury suffered while parking the car, or, a mechanic giving a covered auto a test drive after repair work could be an insured and receive medical payments if injured in an accident. This particular exclusion prevents such individuals from receiving medical payments under the named insured's CA 99 03.

It is curious that the above exclusion has an exception for insureds who are working in a business of selling, servicing, repairing or parking autos if that business belongs to the named insured. After all, CA 99 03 still has an exclusion that applies to bodily injury to the named insured's employees and that would seem to negate the exception. For example, if the named insured is an auto repair shop, and an employee is injured while driving a covered auto, he or she is not entitled to med pay coverage, due to the employee exclusion. How can an insured work in a business that belongs to the named insured and not be an employee of the named insured? A CEO maybe, or a partner? In any case, insureds need to know that even if one exclusion does not apply, there may be another one to consider before medical payments can be claimed.

Bodily injury caused by declared or undeclared war or insurrection or any of their consequences is excluded under CA 99 03.

Bodily injury to anyone using a vehicle without a reasonable belief that the person is entitled to do so is excluded. The key element here is the phrase "reasonable belief." The phrase is not defined on CA 99 03 and so, is subject to interpretation.

Reasonable Belief for Auto Use—Two Scenarios

The named insured on a business auto policy is an individual. His family members include a teenage son who has permission to use the covered auto on weekends. One weekend, the son was driving with friends to a party. After the party, the son was intoxicated and in no condition to drive so he allowed his girlfriend to drive the car. An accident occurred and the girlfriend was slightly injured. The named insured wanted to pay her medical costs but the insurer declined, stating that she did not have a reasonable belief that she was entitled to drive the car. The insured did not explicitly give her permission to drive his car, but couldn't she believe she was allowed since the son, also an insured under the med pay form, let her drive?

The exclusion on the med pay form speaks about the person using the car not having a reasonable belief that he or she is entitled to do so; it does not declare that permission from the named insured or any other insured is required before someone is allowed to use the car. The wording on the med pay endorsement creates, therefore, a subjective intent, in that, if the user reasonably believes he or she is entitled to drive the car, the exclusion does not apply. The permission of the named insured is not relevant in this case. Besides, the son is an insured under the terms of the endorsement and he allowed the girl to drive. So, if the insurer wants an insured to have given permission to the driver before the reasonable belief exclusion can be dropped, it happened. The medical expenses should be paid to cover the girl's injuries.

The named insured is a corporation that allows employees to drive company cars home and use them for personal purposes. There are no restrictions on the use of these cars except that the employees are expected to use the cars "prudently."

An employee with one of these company cars never specifically told his family members they could or could not use the car, although his wife and 18-year old daughter had used the car in the past to run errands and go shopping. A problem arose when the 13-year old son took the car, without the knowledge of the father, and had an accident. The employee told the company about the accident and a med pay claim was put in for the medical expenses of the son. The company said the son was an insured

(scenario continues next page)

> *(continued from previous page)*
>
> *since he was occupying a covered auto; the insurer said the boy could not possibly have a reasonable belief that he was entitled to use the car, so there was no coverage. The employee said that since his wife and daughter used the car, the son probably thought he could too. Isn't this reasonable belief?*
>
> The insured could make a case that the son had a reasonable belief that he could use the car since other family members used it, if the son had a driver's license. However, until state law allows 13 year olds to get a driver's license and drive alone, there is no rational basis to support the proposition that the son had a reasonable belief that he could drive the car. Reasonable belief can be subjective, but it also has to be reasonable. Permission to drive on the public roads is a privilege granted and controlled by the state, and a 13 year old should have no misconceptions that he is allowed to drive. The boy is old enough to know he should not be driving.

The final exclusion on CA 99 03 deals with bodily injury sustained by an insured while occupying a covered auto used in any professional racing or demolition contest or stunting activity, or while practicing for such a contest or activity. The exposures of professional racing or stunt car driving or demolition derbies are, by their very nature, more appropriately handled by a specially written policy and not the BAP or its endorsements. This exclusion accomplishes that task.

Limit of Insurance

Regardless of the number of covered autos, insureds, premiums paid, claims made or vehicles involved in the accident, the most the insurer will pay for bodily injury is the limit shown in the declarations. But, this limit is for each insured injured in any one accident. In other words, the insurer will pay the medical expenses of each injured insured up to the limit shown in the declarations form. If there are five insureds in a covered auto and they are injured in the same accident, and the med pay limit is $5,000, each injured insured can have up to $5,000 of his or her medical expenses (or funeral expenses) paid. Furthermore, paying a claim under this form does not reduce the limit of insurance shown. So, if the five insureds injured in the first accident are injured again two weeks later in a second accident, the $5,000 limit is available for each of them once again.

The limit of insurance clause also declares that no one is entitled to receive duplicate payments for the same elements of loss under the med pay form and any liability coverage form, uninsured motorists coverage, or underinsured motorists coverage. For example, if an injured person can get paid for the injuries suffered in an auto accident from the liability coverage section of the BAP, then that person will not be entitled to get paid for the same injuries under the medical payments coverage. The insurer wants to make sure that the injured person is not paid twice (or more) for the same injury arising from the same accident. This language corresponds with that found in the limit of insurance clause in the liability coverage section of the BAP in order to strengthen the case against duplicate payments.

Changes in Conditions

CA 99 03 offers two changes to the conditions section of the business auto policy.

The first change is that the transfer of rights of recovery condition does not apply to the med pay coverage. This makes sense in that med pay is not based on liability. A transfer of rights of recovery suggests that one party has a liability claim against another party. Since that concept is not relevant to med pay coverage, the transfer of rights clause can be removed without affecting coverage.

The second change notes that the other insurance clause (in reference to medical payments), when it speaks of "other collectible insurance", applies only to other collectible auto medical payments insurance. CA 99 03 is for medical payments, and so it is only fitting that other insurance that could be applied to the injuries covered by CA 99 03 also be medical payments insurance. Besides, this reinforces the "no duplicate payments" language in the limit of insurance clause discussed earlier. Remember, in that clause, medical payments and liability coverage payments were not to apply to the same elements of loss; this other insurance condition on CA 99 03 also associates medical payments under CA 99 03 with only other medical payments insurance.

Additional Definitions

The definitions found within the BAP are also applicable to endorsement CA 99 03. This "additional definitions" section of the endorsement adds two more that are more closely associated with medical payments coverage than with the coverages found on the business auto policy.

The term family member is defined as a person related to the named insured by blood, marriage, or adoption who is a resident of the named insured's household, including a ward or foster child. As noted previously in this chapter, if the named insured is a corporation or a partnership, the term "family member" is not really relevant. However, if the named insured is an individual, CA 99 03 extends coverage to family members, so the term needs to be defined so as to identify the scope of the coverage.

The other defined term is "occupying." It means in, upon, getting in, on, out or off. This is relevant in that who is an insured under CA 99 03 includes the named insured and family members "occupying" any auto, and anyone else "occupying" a covered auto. The insurer is trying to cover all the bases here by using just about any word that might describe and include "occupying".

The idea behind this definition is to link the injured person with an auto in some way. Medical payments coverage under CA 99 03 is, after all, auto medical payments and it is not an unwarranted idea for the insurer to try to make the payments based on a connection to an auto. For example, if an insured parks the covered auto in a customer's lot and walks into the building, and then gets hurt in some accident, it is not reasonable to expect an auto medical payments policy to apply to that situation.

There may be concern that if an insured has parked his or her car and has walked away from it, and is then struck by another car, the insurer will deny med pay coverage because the insured is not "occupying" the car. However, the named insured and family members are insureds if struck by an auto while pedestrians; so that concern does not apply.

As for anyone else, admittedly, the situation is not as clear cut. If someone other than the named insured or a family member has parked the car and has walked away, how far away from the car does he or she have to be before that person is not considered as getting out of the car? The answer has to be subject to the facts of each individual case. However, due to the fact that medical payments coverage is usually founded in an attempt by the insured to engender goodwill and that the limits of insurance are usually small, it is not unreasonable to suggest that few disputes arise over whether an insured (other than the named insured or a family member) walking away from a covered auto is getting out of that car.

8

Nonownership Coverage

Some insured businesses have a liability exposure due to the use of nonowned autos. For whatever reason, some businesses have no need to own autos for business purposes, but do need the use of autos in their every day business activities. For example, a retail store or a delicatessen might need an auto to deliver items to customers, but the need is not so great as to justify the expense of owning a car; the use of employees' cars handles the need. Also, a company may have its officers or employees fly to other cities where they may need the use of rented or hired cars to carry on business.

Many years ago, this nonowned auto exposure was covered by attaching an endorsement to the comprehensive general liability policy. The endorsement, GL 04 19, hired automobile and nonowned automobile liability insurance, applied to the use of any nonowned auto or the use of hired autos in the business of the named insured. Currently, this type of exposure is excluded from the commercial general liability (CGL) coverage forms and is supposed to be covered under the commercial auto program.

The business auto coverage form uses symbols 8 and 9 to denote hired autos and nonowned autos respectively as covered autos for insurance purposes. If these symbols are chosen by the insured, then the business auto policy will provide the sums that an insured legally must pay as damages because of bodily injury or property damage caused by an accident that results from the use of the hired and nonowned autos.

Symbols 8 and 9 were discussed in Chapter 2, but in connection with the description of covered auto designation symbols. This chapter examines symbols 8 and 9 on their own, along with some coverage issues that accompany them.

Automobile leasing or rental concerns and "drive other car" coverages also deal with hired or nonowned autos, but those issues will be discussed in subsequent chapters.

Hired or Borrowed Autos Coverage

If an insured uses a hired or borrowed auto, he or she can be liable for injuries or damages to members of the public as well as to the owner of the hired or borrowed car.

When it comes to physical damage to the hired or borrowed auto, the insured can look to the physical damage coverage section of the BAP for coverage. The insured may be liable for the damage done to the car, but the care, custody, or control exclusion in the liability section of the BAP acts to nullify any liability coverage. However, the physical damage coverage section does offer to pay for loss to a covered auto. So, the insured simply needs to choose the correct symbol from the covered auto designation symbols to make the hired or borrowed auto a covered auto, and put that symbol next to the physical damage coverage he or she desires. The BAP makes such physical damage coverage primary in that the hired or borrowed auto is deemed to be an auto owned by the named insured according to the conditions of the BAP.

As for liability for bodily injuries or property damage to property (other than to the borrowed or hired auto itself), the BAP will provide coverage if the insured chooses the right symbol and places it next to the liability column on the declarations form; symbols 1 or 8 will provide liability coverage for hired or borrowed autos. Such liability coverage is excess over any other collectible insurance. However, there are exceptions to this excess coverage.

First, the other insurance must be collectible. For example, if the insured borrows a car from a neighbor to make a quick pickup of a business article and has an at-fault accident, the hired auto coverage on the insured's BAP will provide liability insurance for him or her. If for some reason the neighbor has no insurance on the auto, the insured's BAP will provide primary coverage should someone make a claim against the insured.

Second, if the insured has hired an auto and, as part of the contract, the insured assumes the liability of the person or entity from which the auto was hired, the BAP provides liability coverage on a primary basis. The assumption of liability has to be part of an insured contract as defined on the BAP.

The third exception that allows primary coverage for hired or borrowed autos is an endorsement to the business auto policy that changes the status of the hired or borrowed auto to that of an owned auto. There are a couple of endorsements that can accomplish this: CA 20 01 and CA 99 16.

CA 20 01 is titled "Lessor—Additional Insured and Loss Payee" This endorsement's main thrust is to make a lessor an insured under the lessee-insured's business auto policy. However, the endorsement also declares that the leased auto described in the endorsement's schedule is considered a covered auto owned by the named insured and not one hired or borrowed. In addition, CA 20 01 provides owned auto status to any substitute, replacement, or extra auto needed to meet seasonal or other needs, under a leasing or rental agreement that requires the named insured to provide direct primary insurance for the lessor. Both declarations transform the leased auto into an auto owned by the named insured for purposes of primary coverage under the named insured's BAP.

CA 99 16, "Hired Autos Specified as Covered Autos You Own," is a rather short endorsement to the auto policy that declares that any auto described in the schedule is considered a covered auto owned by the named insured. As with the previous endorsement, this status change makes the named insured's BAP primary coverage for the hired auto.

Now, the named insured is an insured for any covered auto. If symbol 1 or 8 has been chosen by the named insured to describe the covered auto, then the named insured is an insured for the use of the hired or borrowed auto. If the named insured hires an auto for the use of its employees who are on a business trip, and an auto accident occurs, the named insured's BAP will provide insurance coverage for the named insured (unless some exclusion applies, of course). If the named insured borrows a car from someone or some entity and an auto accident occurs, the BAP, again, will provide insurance coverage for the named insured. However, there are some precautions to take note of.

First, the hired or borrowed auto is not going to be considered a covered auto under symbol 8 if the named insured hires or borrows the car from an employee, a partner, a fellow member of a limited liability company, or from members of their households. So, if the car borrowed or hired in the previous paragraph is borrowed or hired from, for example, an employee of the named insured, the BAP will not consider the car a covered one (under symbol "8"), and the named insured will not have coverage under his or her own business auto policy.

Second, even though the named insured is an insured for the use of the hired or borrowed auto, the owner or anyone else from whom the car is hired or borrowed is not considered an insured. So, if the named insured hires an auto for the employees to use on a business trip, the entity who owns that auto is not an insured under the named insured's BAP. The business auto policy does allow one exception: the owner or anyone else from whom the named insured has hired or borrowed a covered auto is an insured if the covered auto is a trailer connected to a covered auto owned by the named insured. There are endorsements that make the owner of the hired auto an insured under the named insured's BAP, but the basic unendorsed business auto policy will not do so.

Third, symbol 8 calls for the named insured to lease, hire, rent, or borrow a car. If an employee or a partner (who is not a named insured) rents a car in his or her own name or borrows a car, that car is not a covered auto under symbol 8. Even if the car is used on company business, symbol 8 does not consider a covered auto one that is rented or borrowed by someone other than the named insured.

> ## Is Symbol 8 the Proper Symbol for Coverage?
>
> *The named insured is ABC Corporation. The corporation's CEO leases his own auto to the named insured for use on business. And, when he travels, the CEO often rents cars on his own credit card and is reimbursed later from the company for his expenses. The named insured's auto policy uses symbol 8 for liability coverage since it has no owned autos.*
>
> *Recently, a coverage question has arisen. A new company risk manager told ABC's CEO to check the BAP's language describing hired auto coverage because of possible coverage gaps. Is symbol 8 the proper symbol to use in these situations involving the CEO?*
>
> There are two entities here to consider when it comes to the question of coverage under the named insured's BAP: the named insured corporation and the CEO. If the named insured leases the CEO's auto, then symbol 8 makes the leased auto a covered auto and the named insured is an insured for liability coverage under the terms of the BAP. The CEO is not an insured under the BAP since he owns the car. If the CEO rents a car on his business travels in his own name, then neither the named insured nor the CEO are insureds under the BAP. Symbol 8 calls for the named insured to lease, hire, rent, or borrow an auto; it makes no allowances for CEOs, employees, or anyone else to do the hiring or borrowing.
>
> So, there are coverage gaps, but there also are various ways to fill those gaps. If the named insured leases the CEO's car, the CEO can be scheduled as an insured under the BAP through the use of endorsements, such as CA 99 16 (named autos specified as covered autos you own) or CA 20 01 (lessor—additional insured and loss payee). As for the CEO leasing a car for his travels, he needs to rent it in the named insured's name. Or, the named insured can start using symbol 9—nonowned autos— on the BAP; this symbol describes a covered auto as one not owned, leased, hired, rented or borrowed by the named insured as long as the car is used in connection with the named insured's business.
>
> Symbol 9 gives the named insured coverage under the BAP when the CEO rents a car in his own name. However, the CEO may still have a problem under that symbol. The BAP declares anyone an insured while using, with the named insured's permission, a covered auto that the named insured owns, hires, or borrows. If the CEO has rented the car, the named insured has not actually hired or borrowed the car. So, the CEO will not be considered an insured under the company's BAP.
>
> To remedy this, consider endorsement CA 99 33. This endorsement is titled "Employees as Insureds" and makes any employee of the named insured an insured while using a covered auto that the named insured does not own, hire, or borrow in the business of the named insured. As long as the CEO can be considered an employee of the named insured corporation, CA 99 33 will provide coverage for him if he rents a car in his own name and drives it on a business trip. Of course, whether an executive officer
>
> *(scenario continues next page)*

> *(continued from previous page)*
> can be considered an employee depends on the circumstances, since an executive can act as an employee or at other times as an officer of the corporation; but, renting a car and driving it on company business most probably is the act of an employee.

Hired Autos Rating Information

For hired autos rating purposes, a lot depends on whether the insured renter or the owner of the hired car is providing primary coverage. If the insured renter or lessee is providing primary coverage, the auto is rated as though it were owned by the insured renter. If the car owner is providing primary coverage, the premium for the insured renter is figured by applying a company rate per $100 of the cost of hire to the estimated cost of hire for each state of operations and then applying a company rate factor (to account for the primary liability coverage); the resulting premiums for each state should then be combined. The rates and amounts and factors should all be listed in item four of the business auto declarations form.

If cost of hire can not be estimated, as for a small firm that does not anticipate hiring or borrowing autos but desires the coverage nevertheless, the minimum premium is charged and language such as "if any" is inserted in the schedule of hired auto premiums.

For the physical damage coverage on hired autos, one must first estimate the annual cost for the hire of autos for each state where the insured does business and believes it will be hiring autos. Then, after determining the types of coverage desired, a company rate per each $100 annual cost of hire is applied and the premium is established. The total cost of hire for each state has to be added together. This information is also inserted in item four of the declarations form.

Nonownership Liability Insurance

If the insured wants auto nonownership coverage, he or she must choose either symbol 1 (any auto) or symbol 9 (nonowned autos only) for use on the BAP. For any covered auto that the named insured does not own, the BAP is excess over any other collectible insurance.

Symbol 9 designates as a covered auto an auto that the named insured does not own, lease, hire, rent, or borrow that is used in connection with the business of the named insured; this includes autos owned by the named insured's employees, partners, fellow limited liability company members, and members of their households, but only while used in the business or personal affairs of the named insured.

Some businesses may not see the need for auto nonownership coverage; no employees or partners or anyone connected with the company uses a car on company business. However, even if the exposure of the insured to an auto nonownership loss is remote, a loss can still be devastating. For example, the named insured usually uses the U.S. mail or UPS to deliver its packages to customers. One day, after the mail and UPS have stopped picking up for the day, the insured has a package that needs to be delivered to a customer right away. Another customer is in the office and volunteers to deliver the package since it is on his way home. That customer drives off in his own car, has an at-fault accident and kills two people. The family of those two sues the driver and, when it learns the driver was delivering a package for the insured company, sues the company. A multimillion dollar award is given to the family. The driver has only minimum financial limits on his auto policy. Chances are, the claimants will be looking to the insured company for the rest of the money. And, without auto nonownership liability insurance, the insured company is in deep financial trouble.

So, for practical business purposes, any insured company should, at the very least, explore its auto nonownership liability risks. If the risks are small, nonownership insurance can be written on an "if any" basis for a small premium; if the risks are apparent and not so small, the coverage can be purchased for a reasonable amount.

As noted above, nonownership liability coverage can be secured through the use of symbol 1 or symbol 9 on the business auto policy. Symbol 1 is "any auto" and there is no distinction made between owned autos and nonowned autos when it comes to *covered autos*. Symbol 9 is more specific and deserves more comment.

The description of nonowned autos under symbol 9 states that the symbol *includes* autos owned by employees, partners, and members of a limited liability company. This description is not an exclusive list. For example, if an employee drives any car not owned, hired, or borrowed by the named insured—perhaps the car of a neighbor or a friend—and an accident results in a claim being made against the named insured employer, symbol 9 will provide coverage for the named insured. And, consider if the named insured is a nonprofit organization that has many volunteers, these volunteers may often use their own cars in the business of the named insured; nonowned auto coverage will protect the named insured organization if a volunteer is involved in an accident while on the business of the named insured.

Another point to remember is that the coverage under symbol 9 applies on a blanket basis. There is no requirement, as there is for symbol 7 for example, that restricts coverage to autos specifically described in the policy or to newly acquired autos only under certain conditions. Any auto fitting the description under symbol 9 on the BAP is a covered auto for the named insured.

In addition to symbols 1 and 9, there is another provision on the BAP that provides auto nonownership coverage. Any auto that the named insured does not own while used with the permission of its owner as a temporary substitute for a covered auto that is out of service is a covered auto for liability purposes. Of course, the named insured must have already purchased liability coverage under the BAP, and the covered auto must be out of service because of its breakdown, repair, servicing, loss, or destruction. For example, if the named insured is an individual and has his or her car in a garage for repair work, and that garage allows the named insured to drive a garage-owned car while the repairs are going on, the named insured has auto nonownership liability coverage for the use of the garage's car. It makes no difference what symbol the named insured has used to make his or her owned auto a covered auto; this provision in the BAP applies as long as the insured has purchased liability coverage.

Who is an Insured for Nonownership Coverage?

When nonownership coverage is purchased by the named insured, the named insured is, of course, an insured for any nonowned auto since such an auto is a covered auto. But, what about those other than the named insured? If the named insured hired or borrowed an auto, then anyone the named insured allowed to use such a car would be an insured. But, a nonowned auto, by description under the terms of the BAP, does not include autos owned, hired, rented, leased, or borrowed by the named insured. So, how does a driver of such a nonowned car become an insured under the named insured corporation's BAP? There are some limited possibilities.

Endorsements can be added to the BAP naming the drivers as insureds. For example, CA 99 33 makes any employee of the named insured an insured while using a covered auto that the named insured does not own, hire, or borrow in its business or personal affairs. CA 99 17 makes a family member an insured for nonowned autos while being used by the family member, under certain circumstances. CA 99 10 makes any individual named in the endorsement's schedule (and his or her spouse) an insured while using a nonowned auto. Finally, manuscripted endorsements or company-specific endorsements may be available to enable the named insured to extend the auto nonownership coverage to those using the nonowned cars.

The limitations on finding coverage under the named insured's BAP for drivers of nonowned cars stems from the unknown exposures involved. Employees or officers of a corporation can become insureds because they are fairly well known risk factors to an insurer through the use of driving records and company fact sheets. However, if the driver of a nonowned car is a neighbor of the insured corporation's CEO or a customer doing a favor for the named insured, the insurer has no way of knowing the risks involved. Besides, the premium charged for nonownership liability is based on the number of employees and the number of partners, so it is clear that unexpected, unknown drivers are not the focus of attention by insurers providing auto nonownership liability coverage. Business auto insurers would no doubt prefer that such drivers provide their own auto liability insurance.

Nonownership Property Damage Coverage

For some insureds, such as clubs, hotels, restaurants, a major auto nonownership exposure is the driving of autos belonging to members, customers, and other members of the public to and from garages or parking places. Auto nonownership liability coverage under the BAP through the use of symbol 9 will apply to BI or PD for which the insured is liable. And, the exposure also can be partly covered through a CGL form since that form covers the insured's liability for the parking of an auto not owned by or rented or loaned to any insured on the premises owned or rented by the named insured, or on ways next to such premises.

However, liability for damage to the customer's car or the member's car can be excluded if that car is in the care, custody, or control of the insured. Both the BAP and the CGL form exclude this exposure. So, if the insured wishes to insure property damage to autos in its custody, it should purchase garagekeepers insurance, either as a separate policy or through endorsement CA 99 37. Garagekeepers coverage is for sums that the insured legally must pay as damages for loss to a customer's auto left in the insured's care while the insured is parking, servicing, repairing, or storing that auto.

The insured could seek to cover property damage to cars in its care and custody by scheduling symbol 9 next to the physical damage coverages on the BAP declarations form. However, the insured would have to find an insurer willing to write such an exposure and underwriters of commercial auto insurance have in common practice shied away from extending physical damage insurance to nonowned autos. The risk exposures are too great due to the "unknown" factors for insurers to properly underwrite such a coverage.

Rating Information

The commercial lines manual contains rules for determining premium for nonownership liability which are to be used if 50% or less of the insured's employees regularly operate their own cars in the insured's business. Insureds having a higher percentage of employees using their own cars are to be referred to the insurance company for rating.

Item five on the business auto declarations form contains a schedule for nonownership liability. It is based on the *total* number of employees of the insured at all locations; the total number of employees and not just the number who usually use their autos in the insured's business is to be listed. Once this number is set, the premium is selected from the table shown in the state company rates/ISO loss costs for the state where operations are principally conducted.

When a partnership is the named insured, item five has as a rating basis the number of partners. The premium is arrived at by multiplying the private passenger type rates (regardless of the type of autos being used) in the state company rates/ISO loss costs by .10 for each active or inactive partner for the territory in which the partnership is located.

9

Auto Leasing & Rental Coverage

When a business concern leases or rents a car, insurance coverage can be purchased through the use of the BAP and the appropriate choice of the covered auto designation symbol. The insured company can choose symbol 1 (any auto) or symbol 8 (hired autos only) to attain liability and physical damage coverage for the leased car. However, the owner of the leased car is not considered an insured under the lessee's BAP. Now, the lessor can (and should) have its own business auto policy to properly protect its interests; but, there are some endorsements that can be attached to the lessee's BAP and the lessor's BAP that address the legitimate concerns of the lessor. There are a number of endorsements designed specifically for the business of automobile leasing or rental. This chapter offers a discussion of those endorsements.

Lessor—Additional Insured and Loss Payee CA 20 01

CA 20 01 modifies the lessee's business auto policy. This endorsement accomplishes several things. The leased auto described in the schedule is considered a covered auto that the named insured (lessee) owns; this, of course, allows for the named insured's BAP to provide primary insurance coverage. CA 20 01 also makes the lessor named in the schedule an additional insured under the named insured's BAP, allowing that lessor to have the benefit of the coverages afforded to each insured under that BAP. CA 20 01 adds a loss payable clause to the BAP in recognition of the fact that at least two entities have an interest in the leased auto. Through the endorsement, the insurer agrees to pay the financial interest of the named insured and the lessor for loss to a leased auto. The interest of the lessor is obvious — it owns the car. Whether the car is already paid for, or, the lessor still is making payments, the lessor has a definite financial interest in the car which needs to be protected. Whatever interest the named insured has in the car is considered also, but the main thrust of this clause is for the interests of the lessor.

The loss payable clause also has a warning for the lessor. If the loss to the car results from fraudulent acts or omissions on the part of the named insured, CA 20 01 declares that the interest of the lessor is not covered. The named insured's BAP voids the coverage form in any case of fraud by the named insured, so this endorsement attempts to apply a similar message to the lessor. Unfortunately, the wording of this clause can make the lessor an innocent victim of the named insured's fraudulent acts; ideally, the lessor has provisions in the leasing agreement with the lessee to protect it in such cases.

CA 20 01 does have some good news for the lessor in the area of policy cancellation. If the insurer or the named insured cancels the BAP, notice will be sent to the lessor. The common policy conditions form only requires cancellation notice to the first named insured; so this clause enables the lessor to know if the insurance policy it believes exists and which it, no doubt, counted on when it agreed to lease the car, still is in force.

Finally, CA 20 01 notes that the lessor is not liable for the payment of the policy premium; the named insured is the responsible party.

Contingent Liability Coverage CA 20 09

This endorsement protects the lessor in case the insurance required by the leasing agreement is not collectible. For example, if the lessee signs a lease with the lessor that requires $100,000/$300,000/$25,000 policy limits, but for some reason, the insurance is not collectible when an accident occurs, CA 20 09 provides liability coverage and any required no-fault insurance. This protects the lessor in case it is sued as the owner of the car involved in the accident and as the "deep pocket" for coverage because the lessee has no insurance money available for the claimants.

CA 20 09 is an endorsement to the lessor's BAP and provides the coverage noted in the previous paragraph. It applies if the lessee or rentee has furnished the lessor with a certificate of insurance or a copy of the auto policy making the lessor an additional insured on the lessee's or rentee's policy, and, as noted, such insurance is not collectible. CA 20 09 provides to the lessor the lesser of the limits of liability required by the leasing agreement or the amount shown in the endorsement's schedule. For the lessee, the limit of insurance available is the minimum limit required by the state financial responsibility law.

If the lessee's or rentee's policy is cancelled, this endorsement ends on the earlier of the following dates: the date the lessor regains custody of the leased auto, or 30 days after the effective date of cancellation. This clause assumes that the lessor has taken steps to make sure it knows of the cancellation. This is only proper since knowledge of the cancellation should be a business requirement on the part of the lessor, and can be handled through endorsement to the lessee's BAP or through the lease contract language.

Conversion, Embezzlement, or Secretion Coverage CA 20 10

This is an endorsement that can be attached to the lessor's business auto policy to protect it from a loss to its owned car through conversion, embezzlement, or secretion. Comprehensive coverage or specified causes of loss coverage does give the insured coverage for loss to a covered auto due to theft. However, with this endorsement, the insurer is trying to distinguish among the different types of theft.

The theft exposure is usually thought of as an outsider who did not have prior possession of the auto stealing that auto — maybe by "hot wiring" the car. However, a large part of the theft exposure for an auto leasing or rental firm is based on the fact that a lessee or rentee has voluntary possession of the car; in other words, the insured lessor has given the lessee permission to take possession of the car and is trusting that the lessee will voluntarily return it. This type of theft creates a more uncontrollable exposure and the normal theft premium from the BAP is not adequate to cover the risk of loss.

Endorsement CA 20 10 was developed to enable the insurer to charge a premium more in line with the exposure of loss by conversion, embezzlement, or secretion. It begins by adding an exclusion to the physical damage coverage part of the BAP. The exclusion is for loss due to theft, conversion, embezzlement, or secretion by any person in possession of a covered auto under two circumstances: under a bailment lease, conditional sale, purchase agreement, mortgage or other encumbrance; or as a rentee or lessee of such covered auto. So, if the lessee takes possession of the car under a lease agreement and drives off, never to return, the loss to the lessor's car is excluded.

Then, in order to provide the coverage, but at an appropriate premium, CA 20 10 goes on to declare that the exclusion does not apply to covered autos designated in the schedule for which an additional premium is shown. The schedule enables the insured to schedule all its autos or specifically designated autos as covered autos.

The coverage provided by CA 20 10 is for 75% of the actual cash value of the covered auto at the time of the loss, reduced by the amount of any deposit secured by the named insured from the rentee or lessee. If the lessor requires a security deposit from the lessee upfront, it is reasonable that the insurer will take that into consideration when paying a loss to a covered auto;

the insured has the money and if this were not recognized in the payment of a loss, the insured would be receiving somewhat of a double payment. However, the reasoning behind the 75% amount is not as clear. Perhaps this is the insurer's way of trying to get the insured to enact strict leasing guidelines that will serve to prevent a conversion or embezzlement type of loss. In other words, make the insured share in the loss, so as to encourage it to use caution and good business sense in its leasing practices which should, in turn, reduce or prevent such losses.

CA 20 10 has a series of duties it requires of the insured if there is a loss. The named insured must promptly notify the police and, as soon as practicable, notify the insurer or its agent. The insured must cooperate in prosecuting any person whose acts result in the loss, whether the insured wants to press charges or not. The insured must submit a proof of loss, if required, and the insured must make every reasonable effort to locate the covered auto. If the insured locates the car, the insured is to take possession of the car, using legal proceedings if required by the insurer. The insurer promises to reimburse the insured for reasonable expenses in locating and recovering the covered auto.

This last duty deserves comment. The insurer is telling the insured that the insured, not the insurer, has the main task of trying to locate the car. Obviously, the insured should check the addresses, phone numbers, and references listed on the lease application for information as to the whereabouts of the car. If the insured wants to hire a private investigator to locate the car, that can be done. If the insured wants to hire professional repossession agents, that is also acceptable. The only limits the insurer is establishing is that the repossession must be by *legal* proceedings — no breaking into a person's garage or forcing a driver off the road; the expenses of the insured must be reasonable; and, the expenses must be at the request of the insurer or with its consent.

It is sometimes difficult to make a distinction between theft and conversion and embezzlement and secretion. For example, *Black's Law Dictionary (Sixth Edition)* offers the following definitions. "Theft" is defined as the act of stealing or taking of property without the owner's consent. "Conversion" is the unauthorized assumption and exercise of the right of ownership over goods belonging to another, to the alteration of their condition or the exclusion of the owner's rights. "Embezzlement" means the fraudulent appropriation of property by one lawfully entrusted with its possession. "Secretion" means to conceal or hide away, particularly to put property out of reach of another.

These definitions seem to make the point, noted above, that the conversion, embezzlement, or secretion language of CA 20 10 relates to a situation wherein the lost property has been voluntarily given to the taker. The owner of the property, the insured lessor, has willingly handed that property over to another, the lessee or rentee. Subsequently, that property (the auto) has been kept from the owner. At bottom line, a theft to be sure, but, recognizably a different type of theft.

Excluding Autos Under Lease CA 20 11

This endorsement modifies the lessor's auto policy.

A common provision in auto leasing agreements is that the lessee is to provide primary insurance on the leased auto. This coverage must include liability insurance up to the limits specified in the agreement and no-fault coverage if required by state law. The lessee's BAP insures the leased auto and names the lessor as an additional insured. If the lessor chooses to rely wholly upon the lessee's insurance policy, the lessor's BAP can be amended through endorsement CA 20 11. This endorsement excludes liability coverage and any required no-fault insurance for leased autos; that is, any auto that the named insured lessor leases or rents to another under a lease or rental agreement that requires the lessee or rentee to provide primary insurance for the lessor, is not considered a covered auto for liability or no-fault coverages under the lessor's BAP. This accommodates the provisions of the leasing agreement that require the lessee to provide primary insurance, and allows a reduction in premium for the named insured lessor.

If CA 20 11 is used by the lessor, it would be wise to also attach CA 20 09 (discussed previously) to the BAP. If the primary insurance the lessee is supposed to have is not collectible, CA 20 09 gives the lessor the liability coverage and no-fault coverage needed for a claim. CA 20 11 excludes those coverages, and if an accident occurs and the primary insurance that was supposed to be there is not there, the lessor is facing a potentially large claim for which it has no insurance. CA 20 09 acts as backup coverage for the lessor and can ease a risk management concern and still protect the premium savings realized from the use of CA 20 11.

Rent-It-There/Leave-It Here Autos CA 20 12

A normal part of many rental firms' business is receiving one-way rental autos, that is, an auto that a customer rents in one city and drops off at his or her destination in another city. The rented car is not owned by the receiving firm, but a reciprocal business agreement allows it to receive the car, just as one of its cars can be received by another rental firm in another city. This is a convenient business arrangement that benefits auto leasing/rental firms. However, the insurer of an auto rental firm does not intend to cover the owner or the rentee of the auto that its insured is simply receiving and holding for a limited period of time. This intent is accomplished by amending the receiving rental firm's BAP with CA 20 12.

This endorsement declares that the BAP's liability insurance does not apply to the owner or rentee of a rent-it-here/leave-it-there auto not owned by the named insured; a rent-it-here/leave-it-there auto is defined as an auto a rentee rents from someone other than the named insured and leaves with the named insured. CA 20 12 does not diminish the coverage under the BAP for the named insured. If the named insured is named in a lawsuit arising out of the operation of a one-way rental auto that it has received, the named insured will have coverage under its BAP (provided, of course, that the auto qualifies as a covered auto under its BAP). The owner or rentee of the one-way car will have to look to their own respective policies for coverage.

Schedule of Limits for Owned Autos CA 20 13

This endorsement modifies a lessor's BAP.

The typical business entity generally has its auto liability insurance written for one limit of liability on owned, hired or borrowed, and nonowned autos alike. On the declarations form, the limit of insurance for liability coverage is noted and this applies to whichever covered auto symbols the insured has chosen. However, leasing or rental firms often deviate from this practice. For example, a firm may wish to have lower limits on the autos it owns that are used by its employees only, as opposed to higher limits on autos used by rentees and lessees. This is a risk management decision in that the firm can exercise more loss control measures over its own autos and drivers and less control over the autos used by rentees and lessees.

Because the declarations form of the BAP is not suited to showing separate limits of insurance for different autos (if that is what the insured wants), a special schedule of limits endorsement, CA 20 13, is made available to the insured. CA 20 13 allows leasing or rental concerns to schedule different limits of insurance for the following:

1. autos leased or rented to others under an agreement requiring the lessee or rentee to provide direct primary insurance;
2. autos leased or rented under an agreement that does not require the lessee or rentee to provide direct primary insurance; and,
3. autos owned by the named insured and not subject to a leasing or rental agreement.

Each of the first two categories is subdivided as to private passenger autos, commercial autos, and "other." The limit of insurance for each of the categories is on a per accident basis.

Second Level Coverage CA 20 14

This endorsement allows the lessor to arrange insurance coverage under its own auto policy in excess of the limit of insurance that is carried by the lessee, when the lessee is required to provide the primary insurance for a leased or rented car. The lessor can use this endorsement if it feels that perhaps the lessee's primary limits are too low and that some excess insurance can give it peace of mind. By using this endorsement, the lessor insured is saying that, while it is willing to have the lessee provide primary insurance for an auto accident and have the lessor included as an insured on the lessee's policy, it feels the need for excess insurance that will apply to it alone.

CA 20 14 states that the limit of insurance shown in the schedule replaces the limit of insurance shown elsewhere in the policy, or in any lease or rental agreement. The endorsement declares that for the difference between the limit shown in the schedule and the limit shown in any lease or rental agreement, who is an insured does not include the lessee or rentee, the employees, or any person operating an auto with the permission of these people. As an example, the lessee has an auto policy with $50,000 for BI limits; the lessor uses CA 20 14 with limits of $100,000. Even though the lessor is an insured on the lessee's policy and has limits of $50,000 available to it, CA 20 14 allows the lessor to have $100,000 available to it, with $50,000 of that total available to it alone. In other words, the lessor can share the limits on the lessee's policy with the lessee and any other insured, but the lessor has money available to it that is not available to any other insured that may exist under the lessee's policy. CA 20 14 is aimed at preventing any sharing of coverage limits as called for in the other insurance clause of the BAP.

Autos Leased With Drivers—
Physical Damage Coverage CA 20 33

The BAP declares in the Other Insurance clause that any auto that is leased, hired, rented, or borrowed with a driver is not a covered auto. The insured contract definition notes that an insured contract does not include that part of any contract that pertains to the loan, lease, or rental of an auto if the auto comes with a driver. CA 20 33 remedies this lack of coverage to a degree. The endorsement states that for hired auto physical damage coverage, any auto that is leased, hired, rented, or borrowed with a driver, and that is designated or described in the endorsement's schedule is deemed a covered auto. The auto is considered a covered auto that the named insured owns.

Conclusion

These endorsements are standard Insurance Services Office (ISO) endorsements that can be used on a countrywide basis. Some states have state-specific endorsements that reflect changes in terms or coverages as required by state law. Furthermore, individual insurers may have company-specific endorsements that reflect their own underwriting philosophy. Agents and brokers should be aware of any specific endorsements and of differences that may exist between them and the standard ISO endorsements.

10

Drive Other Car Coverage

Drive other car coverage is attained through the use of endorsements to the business auto policy. The purpose of the coverage is, in general, to grant insurance coverage to a driver of an auto that is not owned by either the driver or the named insured.

As an example, the named insured under a BAP is a corporation; it does not own any autos; it allows an executive officer to rent cars in his own name or encourages him to borrow cars when needed, in order to carry out his functions as an officer of the company. Now, in this situation, if the named insured corporation uses symbol 9 — nonowned autos only — to designate covered autos under the BAP, the named insured has insurance coverage, but the executive officer does not. The reason is: symbol 9 designates as covered autos only those autos that the named insured does not own, lease, hire, rent or borrow that are used in connection with the business of the named insured. If the auto is hired or borrowed by the executive officer (who is not the named insured), this meets the description under symbol 9; the car is a covered auto and the named insured is an insured for the covered auto. However, note that the "Who is an Insured" clause on the BAP states that anyone else (besides the named insured) while using with the permission of the named insured a covered auto that the named insured owns, hires, or borrows is an insured. The problem is, by definition, symbol 9 does not include autos owned, hired, or borrowed by the named insured. So, if the named insured's BAP has symbol 9 to designate covered autos, how does the executive officer get to be an insured under his company's BAP if he rents or borrows a car?

The answer is drive other car coverage. This coverage acts to extend the scope of the named insured's auto insurance to include certain scheduled drivers.

Drive Other Car Coverage — Broadened Coverage for Named Individuals CA 99 10

This endorsement attaches to the business auto policy and has a schedule to list the individual(s) who are to be considered insureds as well as the coverages that apply. Available coverages include liability coverage, medical payments coverage, physical damage coverages, and uninsured/underinsured motorists coverage. Such coverages apply only where and when a premium is shown in the endorsement's schedule. CA 99 10 declares that any auto that the named insured does not own, hire, or borrow is a covered auto for liability coverage while being used by any individual named in the schedule, or by his or her spouse while a resident of the same household. The individual named in the schedule and his or her spouse, while a resident of the same household, are considered insureds while using the covered auto. For example, a corporation is the named insured under a BAP; it has CA 99 10 endorsed to the BAP and has named its new CEO on the schedule. The CEO does not own a car so he rents one using his personal credit card. CA 99 10 gives the CEO and his spouse insurance under the corporation's BAP for whichever coverages are noted (and paid for) on CA 99 10.

There are some other important points to note concerning CA 99 10.

The individual named in the schedule is an insured. The spouse of that individual does not need to be named in order to be an insured under CA 99 10; and, there is no additional premium charge for the spouse's coverage. However, the spouse must be a resident of the same household as the named individual. In other words, if the CEO discussed above is divorced or separated from his spouse, that spouse is not an insured under the terms of CA 99 10. Any other person — friend, son, daughter, relative, neighbor — must be named on the schedule in order to be considered an insured under CA 99 10.

The auto used by the named individual can not be owned by the individual. To be a covered auto, that car can be rented or borrowed or leased by the individual, but it cannot be owned by him or any member of his household. The car can even be furnished or available for the regular use of the named individual or spouse, but it cannot be owned by them. Furthermore, the car is not a covered auto if it is used by the named individual or his or her spouse while working in a business of selling, servicing, repairing, or parking autos.

Finally, the auto is a covered auto while being used, and the named individual is an insured while using the covered auto. In other words, the named individual can use the car on business purposes or personal purposes and it fits the criteria for coverage under CA 99 10. So, for example, if the

CEO discussed previously drives the rented car on vacation, endorsement CA 99 10 will sill provide coverage for him.

Endorsement CA 99 10 also offers auto medical payments coverage and uninsured and underinsured motorists coverage provided the premiums are marked on the schedule. If the insured has chosen those coverages, CA 99 10 makes the following change in the "Who is an Insured" clause of the BAP: any individual named in the schedule and his or her family members are insureds while occupying (or while a pedestrian when being struck by) any auto not owned by the named insured. The significant point here is that the coverage is extended to certain other family members of the named individual and not just the spouse. A family member is defined on CA 99 10 as "a person related to the individual named in the schedule by blood, marriage or adoption who is a resident of the individual's household." So, for med pay and UM coverage, sons, daughters, brothers and sisters, mothers and fathers of the named individual are considered insureds under CA 99 10 — as long as they live with the named individual.

The named individual and his or her family members have this coverage as long as the auto they are occupying or struck by is not owned by the named insured or by the individual or family member. So, if the CEO is an occupant in a car owned by his son (who is a resident relative), CA 99 10 will not grant med pay coverage to the CEO if he is injured in an accident.

Endorsement CA 99 10 also provides physical damage coverage, but there are several restrictions.

First, the auto must be a "private passenger type auto." Unfortunately, neither CA 99 10 nor the business auto policy defines the term. However, the commercial lines manual does indicate that a private passenger auto is a four wheel auto of the private passenger or station wagon type. Pickups, panel trucks or vans not used for business are rated as private passenger autos. While this definition is somewhat open to interpretation, it does imply that cars, as opposed to trucks and semi-trailers, are the focus of coverage under CA 99 10.

Second, the auto can not be owned by the named insured, the individual named in the schedule, or by any member of the individual's household. CA 99 10 is geared toward auto *nonownership* coverage.

Finally, the covered auto has to be in the care, custody, or control of the individual(s) named in the schedule or his or her spouse. Here again, a distinction is made between the named individual, the spouse, and others. CA 99 10 provides med pay coverage to family members, but if a family member is driving the car, under the terms of CA 99 10, there is no physical damage coverage. An argument could be raised that the named individual has care and custody of the car since he is the one who has leased it, rented it, or borrowed it, but, in reality, the one who has actual possession of the car at the time of an accident is the one who has custody of it.

Insureds under CA 99 10, as well as agents and brokers, should be aware of the coverage distinctions that exist under CA 99 10 based on just who an insured is.

Individual Named Insured CA 99 17

Drive other car coverage is also provided through the use of endorsement CA 99 17. This endorsement modifies the business auto policy and is geared toward the named insured being an individual and toward providing coverage for that individual's family members. By definition, the spouse of the named insured is automatically considered an insured on the same level as the named insured; that is, the "you" and "your" include the spouse if a resident of the same household.

CA 99 17 offers what is called "personal auto coverage." Under this section of the endorsement, a family member of the named insured is added as an insured for any covered auto that is of the private passenger type and owned by the named insured. The family member is also an insured for the use of autos not owned by the named insured, under certain circumstances:

1. That auto cannot be owned by an family member, furnished or available for the regular use of the named insured or a family member; and,
2. The auto cannot be used in the business of selling, servicing, repairing, or parking autos; and,
3. The auto cannot be of a type other than a private passenger type auto while used by the named insured or family member working in any other business or occupation.

Basically then, this section of CA 99 17 extends auto liability coverage to family members of the named insured. This extension may seem superfluous. After all, under the terms of the business auto policy, anyone using a covered auto owned by the named insured with the named insured's permission is an insured; and, presumably, the named insured allows his family members to drive the autos that the named insured owns. However, CA 99 17 removes the requirement that the use of the auto be with permission. In other words, the family member does not need the permission of the named insured (either explicit or implicit) every time he or she uses a covered auto. This arrangement is of value to families when all the family cars are insured under the named insured's business auto policy and the family members have no personal auto policies to cover their driving exposures.

Note, though, that the extension does not come without limits. The family member must be a person related to the named insured by blood, marriage, or adoption and be a resident of the named insured's household in order to be an insured under CA 99 17. In other words, if the son of the named insured lives with his mother who is divorced from the named insured, and drives a car owned by the named insured, the son is not an insured under CA 99 17 (although, as noted above, the "Who is an Insured" clause on the BAP would make the son an insured as long as he is driving the car with the permission of the named insured). In addition, the auto driven by the family member must be of the private passenger type — no trucks or semis. Note, however, that pick-ups or vans not used for business purposes do qualify as private passenger type autos under CA 99 17.

CA 99 17 makes family members insureds while using nonowned autos also, but the restrictions on that are as noted above.

The endorsement also takes note of physical damage coverage. While any auto that the named insured owns (of the private passenger type) is a covered auto, a nonowned auto can also be considered a covered auto. The nonowned auto must be a private passenger type auto, pick-up, van, or trailer not owned by or furnished or available for the regular use of the named insured or any family member, while in the custody of or being operated by the named insured or any family member. As an example, if a family member gets into a customers car and drives it away from blocking the driveway of the business, the physical damage insurance will apply if the car is damaged and if the named insured's owned autos have physical damage coverage under the BAP. On the other hand, if the nonowned auto is one that is leased or rented by the named insured or a family member, that car is considered a car furnished or available for the regular use of the insureds, and therefore is not considered a covered auto under CA 99 17.

One final note on endorsement CA 99 17. The drive other car coverage provided by this endorsement is at no additional charge if the policy covers a private passenger auto not used for public transportation (e.g. a taxi), or covers a pickup, panel truck, or van not used in the business of the insured (other than for farming or ranching).

11

Endorsements

The business auto policy can be modified in several ways through the use of endorsements. Additional insureds can be added to the policy, exclusions can be added or modified, or existing coverages can be redefined.

The Insurance Services Office (ISO) publishes standard endorsements that can be attached to the BAP. There are also company specific endorsements that reflect an individual insurer's underwriting and risk management philosophy. And, there are manuscripted endorsements that an insurer will produce in order to respond to a particular insured and its specific insurance needs and exposures.

This chapter contains a list of endorsements that ISO publishes, with a brief description of the endorsement and its use with the business auto policy. Note that some endorsements have already been discussed in previous chapters such as the auto medical payments endorsement and the leasing or rental concerns endorsements, so these will not be discussed here.

Some endorsements (usually the standard ISO endorsements) can be added to the policy at no additional charge to the insured. Others require additional premium in order to compensate for the increased exposures that the endorsements create for the insurer.

Mobile Equipment Subject to Motor Vehicle Insurance Laws—CA 00 51

CA 00 51 replaces exclusion 9. on the BAP. This exclusion pertains to bodily injury or property damage arising out of the operations of any equipment listed in certain paragraphs of the mobile equipment definition. CA 00 51 continues this exclusionary language and, in addition, excludes BI or PD or covered pollution cost or expense arising out of the operation of machinery or equipment that is on, attached to, or part of a land vehicle that would qualify under the definition of mobile equipment if it were not subject to a compulsory or financial responsibility law where it is licensed or principally garaged.

CA 00 51 also amends the definition of auto and mobile equipment on the BAP. An auto is now any land motor vehicle, trailer, or semitrailer designed for travel on public roads, or any other land vehicle that is subject to a compulsory or financial responsibility law or other motor vehicle insurance law where it is licensed or principally garaged. And in conjunction with that change, the definition of mobile equipment now states that mobile equipment does not include land vehicles that are subject to a compulsory or financial responsibility law or other motor vehicle insurance law.

The purpose of this endorsement (edition date of December, 2004) is to try to further clarify the difference between an auto and mobile equipment. Confusion often arises when some mobile equipment (for example, a tractor or other farm machinery) can be seen as subject to a state motor vehicle financial responsibility law because the equipment occasionally travels on public roads. Are such vehicles autos or mobile equipment? Will the BAP or the CGL form (or both) respond to a claim involving such a vehicle? CA 00 51 makes the point that any land vehicle that is subject to a motor vehicle financial responsibility law, either by the wording of the law or through a court decision, is considered an auto for insurance coverage purposes. The BAP will respond to a claim based on the ownership or use of such a vehicle; the CGL form will not, since the vehicle is not considered mobile equipment.

Limited Mexico Coverage CA 01 21

CA 01 21 extends the coverage territory to include Mexico, but only for accidents or losses occurring within twenty five (25) miles of the U.S. border, and for trips to Mexico of ten (10) days or less. For example, if the insured businessman drives his covered auto into Mexico to sign a contract and has an accident there, CA 01 21 can provide him with some insurance coverage. Of course, there are limitations.

The insurance provided by CA 01 21 is excess over any other collectible insurance. If a loss to a covered auto occurs in Mexico, the insurer will pay for the loss in the U.S.; the insurer is trying to make sure the repair work is done in the United States. And, the insurance does not apply if the covered auto is not principally garaged and principally used in the United States, or to any insured who is not a resident of the United States.

The endorsement points out that auto accidents in Mexico are subject to the laws of Mexico and that Mexico considers any auto accident a criminal as well as a civil matter. Furthermore, the coverage provided under CA 01 21 may not be recognized by Mexican authorities. The insurer notes that the insured should consider purchasing auto coverage from a licensed Mexican insurance company before driving into Mexico.

It is true that the coverage territory described on the BAP (CA 00 01) does include "anywhere in the world" under certain conditions, and this would include Mexico. However, that clause describes a covered auto of the private passenger type that is leased, hired, rented, or borrowed without a driver for a period of thirty (30) days or less. If, as noted in the example at the beginning of this discussion about CA 01 21, the insured drives his covered auto that happens to be an owned truck into Mexico, the coverage territory extension in the standard BAP will not provide coverage for the insured in case of an accident. The insured needs endorsement CA 01 21 for more proper coverage; of course, buying insurance from a licensed Mexican insurance company, even if only for a day, would be in the best interests of the insured.

Sound Receiving Equipment Coverage — Fire, Police, and Emergency Vehicles CA 20 02

This endorsement modifies the physical damage coverage under the BAP. The BAP excludes loss to audio, visual, or data electronic devices under certain circumstances. CA 20 02 states that the exclusion does not apply to any equipment installed in a covered auto that is owned by a police or fire department, equipped as an emergency vehicle and owned by a political body, or equipped as an emergency vehicle and owned by a volunteer fire department or rescue squad.

The purpose of CA 20 02 is to permit physical damage coverage for items such as two-way mobile radios or scanning monitor receivers regardless of whether or where in a covered auto they are permanently installed, as long as the covered auto is a fire, police, or emergency type vehicle. These types of vehicles are obviously going to have sound receiving equipment due to the nature of the work; and, should an accident or an act of vandalism occur that damages the equipment, the insured wants to know there is coverage without getting into a discussion of whether the equipment is permanently installed or is necessary for the normal operation of the covered auto. This endorsement allows physical damage coverage and is attached to the BAP without a premium charge.

Note that the endorsement provides coverage for the equipment that is installed in covered autos owned by governmental agencies or volunteer departments or squads. The key point here is that the *covered auto must be owned by the governmental agency or volunteer organization*. Many police and fire department personnel and most volunteer rescue or ambulance squad members have sound receiving equipment installed in their own personal cars in order to better respond to emergency situations. This endorsement does not affect their personal cars and will not extend coverage to the equipment, even if used in an emergency situation.

Drive-Away Contractors CA 20 05

If an individual or a company is hired by an auto manufacturer or an auto dealer to drive cars from point A to point B, that individual or company will be held responsible for physical damage to the car and bodily injuries that may result due to an accident; CA 20 05 offers those coverages (for a premium charge). CA 20 05 states that any auto that the named insured does not own, while driven with the plates described in the schedule, is a covered auto, but only while the auto is driven by or for the named insured from its distribution point to its destination. As an example, the ABC car dealership wants several of its cars driven from its location in Cincinnati to another location in Cleveland. The car dealership hires the named insured to drive the cars from Cincinnati to Cleveland. Endorsement CA 20 05 can be attached to the named insured's BAP to give the named insured liability coverage and physical damage coverage while driving the nonowned autos.

This endorsement is similar to the nonowned auto coverage under symbol 9, but there are points of distinction. Nonowned auto coverage applies to any auto that the named insured does not own, lease, hire, rent, or borrow that is used in connection with the named insured's business. CA 20 05 applies only to those nonowned autos that are driven with the registration plates described in the endorsement's schedule. Symbol 9 nonownership coverage applies to the nonowned autos being used anywhere in connection with the named insured's business. Coverage under CA 20 05 requires that the use of the nonowned autos only be from one certain point to another. In other words, CA 20 05 gives nonowned auto coverage, but with restrictions.

Driving Schools CA 20 06

This endorsement provides liability and auto medical payments coverages when a premium is shown in the endorsement's schedule. CA 20 06 declares that any auto not owned by the named insured is a covered auto while being used for driver training. The endorsement also changes the "Who is an Insured" clause of the BAP to include the named insured, any driving instructors, and any student driver while being instructed by the named insured or an instructor.

There are at least two benefits to using this endorsement. It gives the named insured nonowned auto coverage without the use of symbol 9. So, even if the named insured has symbol 2 (owned autos only) or symbol 7 (specifically described autos) on his or her BAP for liability coverage, CA 20 06 will provide nonownership coverage, just in case an employee or the student driver uses his or her own car for driver training. Also, in modifying the "Who is an Insured" definition to include driving instructors and student drivers, CA 20 06 makes sure that those who usually use a covered auto in a driving school business (namely, instructors and student drivers) are insureds under the business auto policy of the named insured. The BAP itself does not grant insured status to those using nonowned autos (except the named insured, of course, under symbol 9); so, CA 20 06 can give the instructors and student drivers some peace of mind while they are driving the training cars, even if the instructors or student drivers own the cars.

The premiums for CA 20 06 are based on the number of driving instructors.

Mobile Equipment CA 20 15

The business auto policy is written to apply to covered "autos." As part of the definition of "auto," it is stated that the definition does not include mobile equipment. However, the insured may, for some reason, want some of its property to be considered as autos for purposes of coverage under the BAP. For example, the named insured may be a general contractor that owns and uses autos, bulldozers, and other road construction machines in its business. Rather than divide coverage between an auto policy and a general liability form and to avoid possible disputes over which insurer covers what item, the insured wants the bulldozers and road construction machines under its auto policy. If the auto insurer agrees, CA 20 15 can be used to accomplish this.

CA 20 15 declares that the vehicles described in the schedule will be considered covered autos and not mobile equipment. The endorsement offers liability coverage, med pay coverage, no-fault and uninsured motorists coverages, and physical damage coverages, for which premiums are charged.

Mobile Homes Contents Coverage CA 20 16

The business auto policy is for covered autos which can include mobile homes (remember, the definition of auto is a land motor vehicle designed for travel on public roads, and that includes motor homes). If the insured has a motor home designated as a covered auto under the BAP, endorsement CA 20

16 gives some coverage for loss to covered property in, attached to, or within 25 feet of the covered auto. The coverage is chosen by the insured and can be just for a fire loss, or limited specified causes of loss, or specified causes of loss (the same as limited specified causes of loss but with mischief or vandalism added); loss due to theft is not covered.

Note that the coverage is for "covered property". Covered property is defined on the endorsement as TV antennas, awnings, and equipment designed to create additional living facilities, and other household furniture or other personal property belonging to the named insured or family members or for which the named insured is liable. So, for example, if the named insured has chosen specified causes of loss coverage for chairs and a refrigerator and bar that he or she has installed in a covered mobile home, and one night a vandal breaks into the mobile home and trashes all the equipment, CA 20 16 will provide coverage for the loss. If the named insured has borrowed a neighbor's portable bar for a trip in the mobile home and the vandalism occurs, CA 20 16 applies since the named insured is liable for that neighbor's personal property. There are some limitations to this coverage, however.

As noted, the covered property has to be in, attached to, or within 25 feet of the covered auto. For example, if the named insured takes the neighbor's portable bar mentioned above out of the mobile home and transports it a mile down the road to another person's mobile home for a party, CA 20 16 will not apply to a loss to the bar. Also, the insured has to choose which coverage he or she wants and pay the premium; if the insured pays only for fire coverage, a vandalism loss will not be covered. The insurance provided by CA 20 16 does not apply to loss to business or office equipment, sales samples, records, currency, coins, deeds, contracts, securities, or stamps. CA 20 16 is basically for living facilities and personal property that makes living in a mobile home more comfortable; business or office equipment and sales samples and, yes, even money do not fit this description. Finally, as noted previously, loss caused by theft is not covered.

CA 20 16 replaces the limit of insurance clause on the BAP's physical damage section with the following: the most the insurer will pay for loss is the smallest of the amount shown in the endorsement's schedule, the actual cash value of the covered property at the time of loss, or the cost of repairing or replacing the covered property with other of like kind or quality.

This endorsement may seem superfluous in that the BAP pays for loss to a covered auto's equipment. However, CA 20 16 can be used to short circuit any argument over whether the property lost is actually "equipment" belonging to a covered auto. And, CA 20 16 will allow coverage for loss to things like tapes, records, and other electronic equipment that the BAP excludes. This is due to the fact that "covered property" is defined under CA 20 16 as including "other personal property belonging to the named insured or for which the named insured is liable". If the named insured has put records or a CD player in the mobile home to increase his or her living comfort level, those items are covered property under the endorsement.

If the insurer does not want to cover loss to such property, it can, of course, decline to attach CA 20 16 to the BAP. Or, it can attach CA 20 17 which states that physical damage coverage for a covered auto that is a mobile home does not apply to: loss to the covered auto's contents, except equipment usual to trucks or private passenger autos; loss to TV antennas, awnings, or cabanas; or loss to equipment designed to create added living facilities.

Professional Services Not Covered CA 20 18

This endorsement changes the liability coverage section of the BAP. It adds an exclusion stating that the insurance does not apply to bodily injury: resulting from the providing or the failure to provide any medical or other professional services; resulting from food or drink furnished with these services; or resulting from the handling of corpses. Such professional services are better handled through professional liability coverage forms in which the exposures can be matched by an adequate premium.

CA 20 18 does not affect any auto medical payments coverage that the insured may have in his or her business auto coverages.

Repossessed Autos CA 20 19

When endorsement CA 20 19 is in force, any auto that the named insured repossesses is considered to be a covered auto, but only while being repossessed by the named insured, held for sale after repossession by the named insured at locations listed in the endorsement's schedule, or pending delivery after sale. The repossessed autos can be insured for liability and physical damage coverages. The premium basis can be on a reporting basis (quarterly or monthly) or on a nonreporting basis, whichever is agreed to by the named insured and the insurer. The insurance provided by this endorsement does not apply to any auto while used for other business or personal purposes; so, if the insured or his employee wants to use the repossessed auto to visit a friend or to run to the diner for lunch, CA 20 19 excludes coverage. Finally, it should be noted that CA 20 19 clearly states that "Who is an Insured" does not include anyone from whom an auto has been repossessed.

Snowmobiles CA 20 21

This endorsement provides insurance coverages for snowmobiles that are described as covered autos on the schedule; the available coverages are liability, medical payments, uninsured motorists (underinsured motorists coverage can be scheduled when such coverage is not included in uninsured motorists coverage), and physical damage. Despite the fact that CA 20 21 allows the insured to describe the snowmobiles to be covered in a schedule, it also takes the opportunity to define "snowmobile". The term means a land motor vehicle that is designed for use on ice and snow and mainly off public roads, and that is propelled only by mechanical means other than airplane type propellers or fans.

CA 20 21 adds several exclusions to the business auto policy. The insurance does not apply to: the snowmobile while in any racing or speed contest or while rented or leased to others by the named insured; under liability coverage, bodily injury to anyone occupying or towed by the snowmobile; loss to the snowmobile resulting from breaking through ice. Some of the exclusions can be deleted by paying an additional premium noted on the endorsement.

The total premium that is stated in the schedule applies for the entire policy period and is not refundable if the named insured cancels the policy.

Registration Plates Not Issued for a Specific Auto CA 20 27

This endorsement is for risks other than auto dealers that possess registration plates not issued for attachment to a specific auto. Something similar was discussed previously under endorsement CA 20 05, drive-away contractors. However, whereas CA 20 05 was for autos that the named insured does not own, CA 20 27 applies to any auto while used with the plates described in the schedule of the endorsement. Furthermore, CA 20 27 provides liability, personal injury protection, med pay, and uninsured motorists coverages, whereas CA 20 05 provides only liability and physical damage coverages. Finally, CA 20 05 provides coverage only while the auto is being driven from one point to another; CA 20 27 has no such limitation.

Autos Leased, Hired, Rented or Borrowed With Drivers — Physical Damage Coverage CA 20 33

Remember that under the business auto policy, any auto that is leased, hired, rented, or borrowed with a driver is not considered a covered auto; CA 20 33 changes that. CA 20 33 declares that for hired auto physical damage coverage, any auto that is leased, hired, rented, or borrowed with a driver will be deemed a covered auto that the named insured owns. The auto has to be described in the endorsement's schedule and a premium has to shown for the coverages chosen (comprehensive, specified causes of loss, collision).

By designating the leased, hired, or rented car to be an auto that the named insured owns, CA 20 33 confirms primary insurance status on such an auto.

Designated Insured CA 20 48

This endorsement allows a designated person or organization to be scheduled as an insured for liability coverage under the business auto policy. Each person or organization indicated on the endorsement's schedule is an insured, but only to the extent that the person or organization qualifies as an insured under the "Who is an Insured" provisions of the BAP. In other words, CA 20 48 can name any person or organization as an insured under the BAP; however, if the "Who is an Insured's provision declares that such a person or organization is not an insured, CA 20 48 does not overrule that declaration. For example, the owner from whom the named insured hires or borrows a covered auto is not an insured according to the wording of the "Who is an Insured" provision. Even if that owner is listed in the schedule of CA 20 48 as a designated insured, he or she will not be considered as an insured under the BAP.

Explosives CA 23 01

This endorsement addresses another type of business activity that demands a specialty type coverage. CA 23 01 declares that the liability insurance of the BAP does not apply to bodily injury or property damage caused by the explosion of explosives that the named insured makes, sells, or transports.

Multi-Purpose Equipment CA 23 03

Endorsement CA 20 15 made the vehicles described in the schedule autos and not mobile equipment. CA 23 03 reverses this and makes the vehicles described in the schedule mobile equipment and not autos.

Rolling Stores CA 23 04

CA 23 04 states that liability coverage for a covered auto that is a rolling store is changed by adding the following exclusion: the insurance does not apply to bodily injury or property damage resulting from the handling, use, or condition of any item that the insured makes, sells, or distributes if the injury or damage occurs after the insured has given up possession of the item. The endorsement does not define "rolling store", but the term probably refers to a vehicle used as a mobile snack bar or lunch van, selling food and drinks to people like construction workers or others where the products are brought to the customers instead of the customers going to a place of business to eat and drink. Using this as an example, if the insured sells a ham sandwich from his rolling store to a construction worker and the worker later gets sick from that sandwich, the business auto policy will not provide coverage for any claim arising out of that incident.

If the insured is in the lunch wagon business, this exclusion will delete the most important products liability coverage that may have existed for the insured under the BAP. It would make sense for an insured in this type of business to have products liability coverage, so a general liability coverage form is a needed supplement to the insured's BAP.

Wrong Delivery of Liquid Products CA 23 05

CA 23 05 adds an exclusion to the liability coverage section of the BAP. The endorsement states that the insurance does not apply to BI or PD resulting from the delivery of any liquid into the wrong receptacle or to the wrong address, or from the delivery of one liquid for another, if the BI or PD occurs after delivery has been completed.

This endorsement seems to be an example of overkill by an insurer. The BAP has a completed operations exclusion that applies to bodily injury and property damage arising out of the work of the named insured after that work has been completed. Therefore, the BAP already excludes coverage for any injuries or damages based on the insured's delivery of oil to the wrong tank or delivery of the wrong fluid to an oil tank. CA 23 05 simply repeats that message.

If the insured wants coverage for this type of exposure, he or she needs a general liability coverage form to complement the coverages afforded under the business auto policy.

Coverage for Injury to Leased Workers CA 23 25

With respect to the employee indemnification and employer's liability exclusion in the liability section of the BAP, CA 23 25 changes the definition of employee so that an employee does not include a leased worker or a temporary worker. This is done, as an example, so that a leased worker can seek damages for bodily injury under the named insured's BAP and not have the claim automatically excluded because the leased worker is considered an employee of the named insured.

The definition of leased worker under the BAP is a person leased to the named insured by a labor leasing firm under an agreement between the named insured and the leasing firm to perform duties related to the conduct of the named insured's business. Now, if the lease agreement or state law or the business protocol of the named insured and the leasing firm mean to look upon the leased worker as an employee of the leasing firm, CA 23 25 implements this notion. The endorsement eliminates disputes that may arise after such a worker is injured as to whether he or she is an employee of the named insured. The leasing firm is the employer; the leased worker is the firm's employee; and the named insured on the BAP has liability coverage in case the leased worker files a claim against him or her.

Public Transportation Autos CA 24 02

This endorsement is for covered autos that are licensed or used to transport the public, such as taxis, limousines, school busses, and van pools. What CA 24 02 does is to modify the care, custody, or control exclusion on the business auto policy so that the exclusion does not apply to property damage to or covered pollution cost or expense involving property of the insured's passengers while such property is carried by the covered auto. CA 24 02 reinforces the fact that common carriers are liable for damage done to their passengers' property, such as luggage or clothing.

Fire; Fire and Theft; Fire, Theft and Windstorm; and Limited Specified Causes of Loss Coverages CA 99 14

This endorsement provides only those coverages where a premium is shown in the schedule. Furthermore, each of the coverages applies only to autos shown as covered autos. CA 99 14 basically replaces the physical damage coverages as listed on the BAP. Instead of the comprehensive, specified causes of loss, and collision coverages, CA 99 14 offers only the causes of loss noted in its title. The insured gets limited physical damage coverage and a lower premium for the limited exposures. Loss is paid on an actual cash value basis or the cost of repair, whichever is less.

Rental Reimbursement Coverage CA 99 23

The business auto policy itself does not provide rental reimbursement to the insured in case its covered autos are out of action and a substitute auto is needed. The BAP does provide temporary transportation expenses due to a theft of a covered auto, but if the car is damaged by fire or vandalism and can not be used by the insured, the BAP will not provide rental reimbursement for substitutes. CA 99 23 offers a remedy for that.

CA 99 23 offers to pay for rental reimbursement expenses incurred by the named insured for the rental of an auto because of loss to a covered auto; no deductibles apply to this coverage. The payment is for those expenses incurred during the policy period beginning 24 hours after the loss and ending with the lesser of the following number of days: the number of days reasonably required to repair or replace the covered auto, or the number of days shown in the endorsement's schedule. The named insured has to choose the physical damage coverages which may cause the loss (comprehensive, collision, or specified causes of loss), choose the autos which will be covered autos, and choose a time period of the number of days it is estimated a rental car will be needed. If the insured has this endorsement and its covered auto suffers a loss due to fire, the insured can rent a substitute car to continue its business activities and get reimbursed by the insurer for the cost of rental.

The coverage under CA 99 23 does not apply while there are spare or reserve autos available to the named insured for its operations. At first glance, this clause is saying that if the named insured has, for example, three or four autos for business use and one or two are put out of commission due to a fire, the insurer will not pay for the rental of any substitute cars. Of course, the insured can argue that it needs its full complement of autos to carry on business as usual, and in that case, this particular clause on CA 99 23 is vague enough to allow coverage for such an instance. For example, if the insured needs its four autos to operate its business normally, and a loss occurs to one of the cars, the insured can say its business would be cut by 25% if it can not have the use of four cars; in other words, the operations of the insured requires the use of four cars. In such a case, the insurer would be wrong to disallow the rental of a fourth car just because the insured has three autos in use. An insurer might argue this point, but common sense and business sense should prevail and allow the insured to keep its business running up to speed by renting a car.

Stated Amount Insurance CA 99 28

This endorsement changes the physical damage coverage limit of insurance provisions on the BAP by stating that the most the insurer will pay for loss is the least of the following amounts, minus any applicable deductible: the actual cash value of the damaged or stolen property as of the time of the loss; the cost of repairing or replacing the damaged or stolen property; or the amount shown in the schedule of CA 99 28. The insured must identify the covered autos, list the coverages desired, and state a limit of insurance in the schedule of the endorsement.

The insured should know that the stated amount endorsement does not guarantee that the stated amount in the schedule is the amount he or she will be paid if the covered auto suffers a loss. The insurer has reserved for itself the right to pay a lesser amount if the situation warrants. As an example, the insured has $5,000 listed in the schedule as the limit of insurance for the covered auto; a fire occurs that destroys the car; the insurance adjuster decides that the car had an actual cash value of $3,000 at the time of the loss; the insurer will pay the $3,000 amount, less the deductible.

Tapes, Records, and Discs Coverage CA 99 30

The business auto policy declares in the physical damage section that the insurer will not pay for loss to tapes, records, or discs. However, the insured can buy back this coverage by using CA 99 30. The endorsement allows payment, under comprehensive coverage, for loss to tapes, records, discs, or other similar devices used with audio, visual, or data electronic equipment. These items must be the property of the named insured or of a family member, and must be in a covered auto at the time of loss; so, for example, if the tapes are borrowed from a neighbor or an employee, or if the tapes are stolen from the insured's office, CA 99 30 offers no coverage. The most the insurer will pay for loss is $200.

Employees as Insureds CA 99 33

CA 99 33 makes any employee of the named insured an insured while using a covered auto that the named insured does not own, hire, or borrow in the business or personal affairs of the named insured. This endorsement contemplates the use by the named insured of symbol 9 — nonowned autos — to designate covered autos under the BAP. Since that symbol includes autos owned by employees that are used in connection with the named insured's business, it is only fitting that the employees be covered under the named insured's BAP. The "Who is an Insured" provisions of the BAP do not extend liability coverage to the employee for the use of nonowned autos; this endorsement accomplishes that.

Social Service Agencies— Volunteers as Insureds CA 99 34

This endorsement changes the "Who is an Insured" provision under the liability coverage section of the BAP. CA 99 34 makes anyone volunteering services to the named insured social service agency an insured while using a covered auto that the named insured does not own, hire, or borrow; the volunteer must be transporting clients of the named insured or transporting other persons in activities necessary to the named insured's business. Also, anyone else who furnishes the auto is an insured.

As an example, if Mrs. Smith, who volunteers at a center for abused women, drives a neighbor to the center for counseling, CA 99 34 will extend liability coverage under the center's BAP to Mrs. Smith. If that auto belongs to the neighbor and the neighbor allows Mrs. Smith to drive the car to the center, the neighbor is also an insured under the center's BAP. The volunteer has to be transporting clients of the named insured or transporting others who are in activities necessary to the named insured's business, so if Mrs. Smith goes to visit her relatives after dropping the neighbor off at the center, the liability coverage of the center's BAP no longer applies. The insurance extended to Mrs. Smith under CA 99 34 is excess over any other collectible insurance since the auto is one that is not owned by the named insured.

Garagekeepers Coverage CA 99 37

This endorsement can be added to a business auto policy to provide garagekeepers coverage (with direct coverage options) to risks that are not engaged in a typical garage operation, such as a business that installs car stereos or car phones. CA 99 37 will give coverage to the named insured for all sums that the insured legally must pay as damages for loss to a customer's auto or equipment while the insured is attending, servicing, repairing, parking, or storing that car.

CA 99 37 adds two definitions to the BAP: garage operations and work you (the named insured) performed. Garage operations means the ownership, maintenance, or use of locations for the purpose of selling, servicing, repairing, parking, or storing customer's autos; it also includes operations necessary or incidental to the performance of garage operations. Work performed by the named insured includes work that someone performed for the named insured.

Also, the definition of auto is changed to reflect the idea of "customer's auto." This makes sense since the coverage under CA 99 37 is for loss to a customer's auto. Customers include the named insured's employees and members of their households who pay for services performed. So, if an employee is having his auto serviced at the named insured's place of business and the car is negligently damaged, CA 99 37 will apply to the loss. Interestingly, there is no exclusion on CA 99 37 that would exclude coverage if the employee was the one working on his own car and damaged it. As long as the insured (the named insured) is legally responsible for the loss to the customer's auto, CA 99 37 provides coverage.

Finally, the definition of "loss" on the BAP is expanded to include "any resulting loss of use," in keeping with the usual garagekeepers coverage.

Exclusion or Excess Coverage Hazards Otherwise Insured CA 99 40

When the named insured does not want liability coverage to apply to certain autos that he or she owns, those autos must be designated in the schedule of CA 99 40 and a provision box must be checked. The insured can choose no liability coverage at all, liability coverage not applying before other insurance ends, or liability coverage applying on an excess basis to the other insurance.

Loss Payable Clause CA 99 44

If the insured still owes money on his or her auto to a bank or credit union, CA 99 44 allows the loss payee bank or credit union to have its interests in the car covered under the named insured's BAP. This endorsement covers the interest of the loss payee unless the loss results from conversion, secretion or embezzlement of the part of the named insured. So, in other words, if the auto is destroyed in a fire, the insurer will pay the named insured and the loss payee for their respective interests; if the named insured hides the car away to keep it out of the reach of the creditor bank or credit union (secretion), CA 99 44 will not pay the creditor for its loss.

If the insurer cancels the policy, CA 99 44 declares that the insurer will mail the named insured and the loss payee the same advance notice.

Employee as Lessor CA 99 47

If the named insured leases, hires, or borrows an auto, that auto can be designated a covered auto under the BAP through the use of symbol 8. Hired autos coverage does not include any auto that the named insured leases, hires, rents, or borrows from an employee. However, if the named insured is so inclined as to lease an employee's auto, endorsement CA 99 47 makes such a designated auto a covered auto that the named insured owns. So, if the named insured wants to lease a car from its employee, symbol 8 should not be used to designate that car as a covered auto; endorsement CA 99 47 should be used.

The coverage provided by CA 99 47 is on a primary basis since the auto is considered as one that is owned by the named insured. The employee who leases his or her auto to the named insured is made an insured under the named insured's BAP.

Pollution Liability — Broadened Coverage CA 99 48

This endorsement changes the pollution exclusion on the BAP, in that paragraph a. of the exclusion applies only to liability assumed under a contract or agreement. Paragraph a. deals with the escape or release of pollutants that are being transported by the insured or that are being stored or treated in or upon a covered auto. In other words, if the named insured is transporting a pollutant and an accident occurs, CA 99 48 would provide coverage for BI or PD that arose from any release of the pollutant. If the named insured had assumed the liability of the pollutant manufacturer while transporting the pollutant, CA 99 48 will not help, and the named insured and the manufacturer will not have insurance for the BI or PD.

The other provisions of the pollution exclusion are not affected by CA 99 48. However, the endorsement does change the definition of "covered pollution cost or expense."

That definition is changed so that reference to pollutants being transported by the named insured or being stored or treated in or upon a covered auto is dropped. The reference in the BAP says that such pollutants are not included in the definition of covered pollution cost or expense. However, since CA 99 48 allows coverage for BI or PD due to the release of such pollutants, it is only logical that such a negative reference be dropped in order to remove any possible point of contention over coverage for a loss due to the transporting of pollutants.

Garagekeepers Coverage — Customers Sound Receiving Equipment CA 99 59

The garagekeepers coverage endorsement (CA 99 37) discussed previously does not cover loss to sound receiving equipment unless it is permanently installed in the dash or console opening. So, if the customer has taken his or her car to the named insured for some servicing and a citizen's band radio or a two-way mobile radio that was in the back seat of the car is damaged by a fire or explosion, CA 99 37 will not pay for the damage. CA 99 59 does offer some coverage for that sound receiving equipment, but the coverage is limited.

The insurer, under CA 99 59, does agree to pay all sums that the insured legally must pay as damages for loss to sound receiving equipment in a customer's auto left in the insured's care. However, that coverage is limited in that the equipment must be permanently installed in the car. Granted, the limitation does not mandate that the equipment be permanently installed in the dash or console opening, but it still has to be permanently installed somewhere in the customer's car in order for there to be coverage. Furthermore, loss due to theft of the equipment is not covered. And, even if the named insured tells the customer that he will take responsibility for the equipment, that equipment is not covered for a theft loss.

CA 99 59 offers comprehensive coverage, excluding theft, and collision coverage. The coverage is based on legal liability, but the insured can buy direct coverage.

Audio, Visual and Data Electronic Equipment Coverage CA 99 60

CA 99 60 declares that the insurer will pay, with respect to a covered auto described on the endorsement, for loss to any electronic equipment that receives or transmits audio, visual, or data signals and that is not designed solely for the reproduction of sound. This coverage applies only if the equipment is permanently installed in the covered auto at the time of loss, or if the equipment is removable from a housing unit that is permanently installed in the covered auto at the time of the loss. Also, the equipment must be designed to be solely operated by the use of power from the auto's electrical system, in or upon the covered auto.

CA 99 60 will cover any accessories used with the electronic equipment, but will not cover loss to tapes, records, or discs.

With respect to the limits of insurance, this endorsement states that the insurer will pay, as a result of any one accident, the lesser of the actual cash value of the damaged or stolen property as of the time of loss, or the cost of repairing or replacing the damaged or stolen property with other property of like kind and quality. An adjustment for depreciation and physical condition will be made in determining actual cash value at the time of loss; and, a deductible shown in the declarations will also be applied in accordance with the deductible provisions of the endorsement.

Loss Payable Clause —Audio, Visual and Data Electronic Equipment CA 99 61

CA 99 61 simply lists a loss payee that will be paid along with the named insured for a loss to audio, visual, and data electronic equipment that has been given coverage through the use of CA 99 60. The insurance covers the interest of the loss payee unless the loss results from conversion, secretion, or embezzlement on the part of the named insured.

Uninsured Motorists Coverage Endorsements

Uninsured and underinsured motorists coverage can be added to the business auto policy by endorsements. Such coverages are issued on a state-by-state basis, reflecting the individual state's laws and regulations. Accordingly, the endorsements are state specific, even though the basic coverage for bodily injury sustained by an insured and caused by an accident is the same for every endorsement.

Appendix A — Commercial Auto Checklist

The following commercial auto checklist is meant to collect basic information about an insured's auto exposures and operations so that the insurance professional can better estimate the risk factors to properly underwrite the account. The checklist enables the insured to tell the insurer exactly what coverages he or she wants. The items listed on the checklist are not all-inclusive, but do offer a source of knowledge from which a mutually acceptable insurance contract can be written.

APPENDIX A

Commercial Auto Coverage Checklist
General Information

Named Insured:
D/B/A:
Address:
City, State:
Phone:
FAX:
e-mail:
Named Insured is a(n):   ☐ Individual   ☐ Partnership
☐ Corporation
☐ Limited Liability Co.
☐ Joint Venture   ☐ Other

General business operations:
States/territories in which insured has operations:
Loss control contact name/phone:

Liability Coverage

___ 1. Are all owned autos (and those under long-term lease) described in the policy? (This is especially important when coverage is arranged for "specifically described autos only".)

___ 2. If insured does not have "any auto" symbol liability coverage, is insurance company willing to provide this type of coverage? Does insured understand the arrangement?

___ 3. Is a deductible advantageous for the insured?

___ 4. Any leased autos? If so, does lease stipulate any insurance requirements not provided by existing insurance?

___ 5. Any possibility of short term rental or borrowed autos? Even if this seems unlikely, hired autos coverage on an "if any" basis should be urged.

___ 6. Do employees, partners, or other agents use their own autos on company business? Even the possibility calls for nonownership liability coverage.

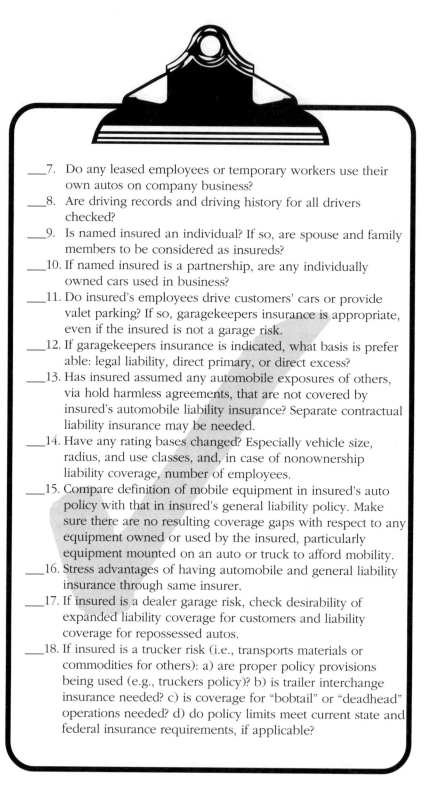

___7. Do any leased employees or temporary workers use their own autos on company business?

___8. Are driving records and driving history for all drivers checked?

___9. Is named insured an individual? If so, are spouse and family members to be considered as insureds?

___10. If named insured is a partnership, are any individually owned cars used in business?

___11. Do insured's employees drive customers' cars or provide valet parking? If so, garagekeepers insurance is appropriate, even if the insured is not a garage risk.

___12. If garagekeepers insurance is indicated, what basis is preferable: legal liability, direct primary, or direct excess?

___13. Has insured assumed any automobile exposures of others, via hold harmless agreements, that are not covered by insured's automobile liability insurance? Separate contractual liability insurance may be needed.

___14. Have any rating bases changed? Especially vehicle size, radius, and use classes, and, in case of nonownership liability coverage, number of employees.

___15. Compare definition of mobile equipment in insured's auto policy with that in insured's general liability policy. Make sure there are no resulting coverage gaps with respect to any equipment owned or used by the insured, particularly equipment mounted on an auto or truck to afford mobility.

___16. Stress advantages of having automobile and general liability insurance through same insurer.

___17. If insured is a dealer garage risk, check desirability of expanded liability coverage for customers and liability coverage for repossessed autos.

___18. If insured is a trucker risk (i.e., transports materials or commodities for others): a) are proper policy provisions being used (e.g., truckers policy)? b) is trailer interchange insurance needed? c) is coverage for "bobtail" or "deadhead" operations needed? d) do policy limits meet current state and federal insurance requirements, if applicable?

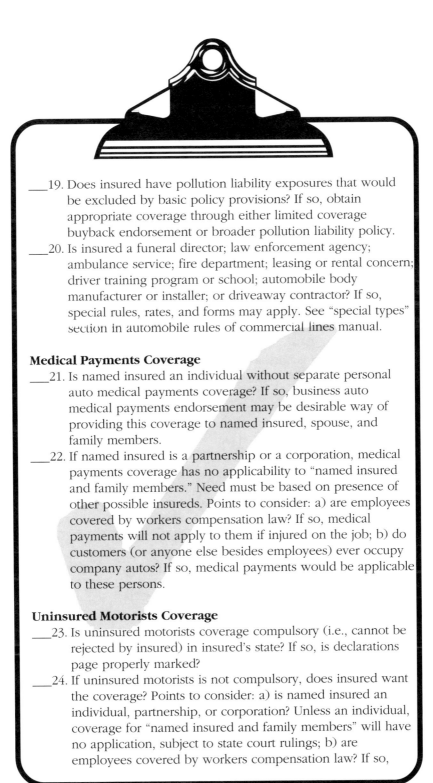

___19. Does insured have pollution liability exposures that would be excluded by basic policy provisions? If so, obtain appropriate coverage through either limited coverage buyback endorsement or broader pollution liability policy.

___20. Is insured a funeral director; law enforcement agency; ambulance service; fire department; leasing or rental concern; driver training program or school; automobile body manufacturer or installer; or driveaway contractor? If so, special rules, rates, and forms may apply. See "special types" section in automobile rules of commercial lines manual.

Medical Payments Coverage

___21. Is named insured an individual without separate personal auto medical payments coverage? If so, business auto medical payments endorsement may be desirable way of providing this coverage to named insured, spouse, and family members.

___22. If named insured is a partnership or a corporation, medical payments coverage has no applicability to "named insured and family members." Need must be based on presence of other possible insureds. Points to consider: a) are employees covered by workers compensation law? If so, medical payments will not apply to them if injured on the job; b) do customers (or anyone else besides employees) ever occupy company autos? If so, medical payments would be applicable to these persons.

Uninsured Motorists Coverage

___23. Is uninsured motorists coverage compulsory (i.e., cannot be rejected by insured) in insured's state? If so, is declarations page properly marked?

___24. If uninsured motorists is not compulsory, does insured want the coverage? Points to consider: a) is named insured an individual, partnership, or corporation? Unless an individual, coverage for "named insured and family members" will have no application, subject to state court rulings; b) are employees covered by workers compensation law? If so,

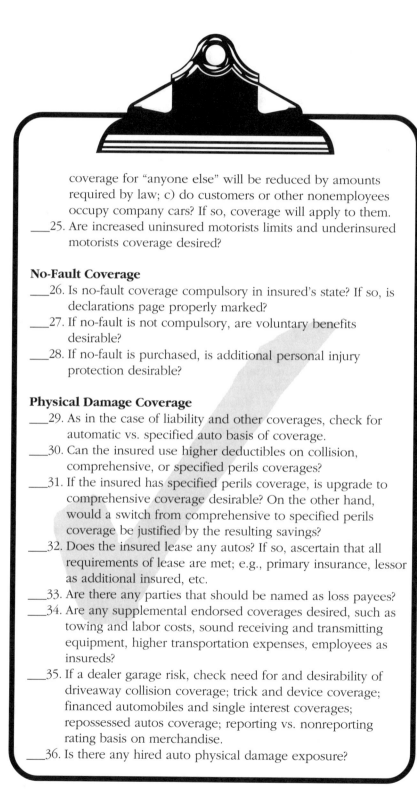

coverage for "anyone else" will be reduced by amounts required by law; c) do customers or other nonemployees occupy company cars? If so, coverage will apply to them.

___25. Are increased uninsured motorists limits and underinsured motorists coverage desired?

No-Fault Coverage

___26. Is no-fault coverage compulsory in insured's state? If so, is declarations page properly marked?

___27. If no-fault is not compulsory, are voluntary benefits desirable?

___28. If no-fault is purchased, is additional personal injury protection desirable?

Physical Damage Coverage

___29. As in the case of liability and other coverages, check for automatic vs. specified auto basis of coverage.

___30. Can the insured use higher deductibles on collision, comprehensive, or specified perils coverages?

___31. If the insured has specified perils coverage, is upgrade to comprehensive coverage desirable? On the other hand, would a switch from comprehensive to specified perils coverage be justified by the resulting savings?

___32. Does the insured lease any autos? If so, ascertain that all requirements of lease are met; e.g., primary insurance, lessor as additional insured, etc.

___33. Are there any parties that should be named as loss payees?

___34. Are any supplemental endorsed coverages desired, such as towing and labor costs, sound receiving and transmitting equipment, higher transportation expenses, employees as insureds?

___35. If a dealer garage risk, check need for and desirability of driveaway collision coverage; trick and device coverage; financed automobiles and single interest coverages; repossessed autos coverage; reporting vs. nonreporting rating basis on merchandise.

___36. Is there any hired auto physical damage exposure?

Special Considerations

___37. Are limits of liability adequate?
___38. Does insured have other insurance, collectible or not?
___39. Has insured ever filed for bankruptcy?
___40. What is the insured's loss history?
___41. Has insured ever been cancelled or non-renewed?
___42. Does insured have an active and effective loss control program?
___43. Any trailers used? Owned and nonowned.
___44. Does insured understand diminution in value exclusion?
___45. Does insured understand duties in event of loss or claim?

Appendix B — Table of Limits

Financial Responsibility and Compulsory Insurance Laws

The laws of all states express the requirement in terms of *split limits*. For example, if the chart shows "25/50/10," the law requires that the policy provide at least $25,000 for bodily injury to each person, $50,000 for all bodily injury, and $10,000 for property damage, each accident.

The insurance laws of some states also state the requirement in terms of a *combined single limit*. For example, if the chart shows "15/30/10 or 40," the law provides that a policy with a combined single limit of at least $40,000 will also satisfy the requirement. A combined single limit of $40,000 means that the insurance will pay up to $40,000 for all bodily injury and property damage arising out of each accident. The required limits for the Canadian provinces are expressed as combined single limits only.

Required Limits, by State

Alabama 20/40/10 or 50
Alaska 50/100/25 or 125
Alberta 200
Arizona 15/30/10 or 40
Arkansas 25/50/25
British Columbia 200
California 15/30/5
Colorado 25/50/15
Connecticut 20/40/10
Delaware 15/30/5
District of Columbia 25/50/10
Florida 10/20/10 or 30
Georgia 25/50/25
Hawaii 25/40/10

Idaho 25/50/15
Illinois 20/40/15
Indiana 25/50/10
Iowa 20/40/15
Kansas 25/50/10
Kentucky 25/50/10 or 60
Louisiana 10/20/10
Maine 50/100/25
Manitoba 200
Maryland 20/40/15
Massachusetts 15/30/5
Michigan 20/40/10
Minnesota 30/60/10
Mississippi 10/20/5

Missouri 25/50/10
Montana 25/50/10
Nebraska 25/50/25
Nevada 15/30/10
New Brunswick 200
Newfoundland 200
New Hampshire 25/50/25
New Jersey 15/30/5
New Mexico 25/50/10
New York 25/50/10*
Northwest Territories 200
North Carolina 30/60/25
North Dakota 25/50/25
Nova Scotia 200
Nunavut 200
Ohio 12.5/25/7.5
Oklahoma 25/50/25
Ontario 200
Oregon 25/50/10
Pennsylvania 15/30/5
Prince Edward Island 200
Puerto Rico
    No F.R. Requirement
Quebec 50**

Rhode Island 25/50/25
Saskatchewan 200
South Carolina 15/30/10
South Dakota 25/50/25
Tennessee 25/50/10
Texas 20/40/15
Utah 25/50/15
Vermont 25/50/10
Virginia 25/50/20
Washington 25/50/10
West Virginia 20/40/10
Wisconsin 25/50/10
Wyoming 25/50/20
Yukon 200

*50/100 for wrongful death.

** Because Quebec has a complete no-fault system for bodily injury, the minimum limit applies only to property damage within Quebec and combined bodily injury and property damage outside Quebec.

Appendix C — Indicators of Vehicle Theft Fraud

Detection – The First Line of Defense

Most claims are legitimate, but some are fraudulent. Therefore, it is appropriate for the adjuster to review all claims for possible fraud. Determining the fraud probability of any claim is facilitated when the adjuster is familiar with various fraud indicators.

These indicators should help isolate those claims which merit closer scrutiny. No one indicator by itself is necessarily suspicious. Even the presence of several indicators, while suggestive of possible fraud, does not mean that a fraud has been committed. Indicators of possible fraud are "red flags" only not actual evidence.

Some claims, although suspicious, may have to be paid for lack on conclusive evidence of fraud; however, they should be referred to NICB for further review.

All vehicle thefts and all sales of total loss salvage sold by your company or left in the possession of the claimant at the time of total loss claim settlement should be reported to the NICB. Total loss salvage should include the current and four preceding model years as well as older model years if the vehicle is an expensive sports car, a truck-tractor, or any other vehicle for manual reporting companies. Electronic reporting companies should report all model years.

Indicators of Fraud Concerning the Insured

Insured:
- has lived at current address less than six months.
- has been with current employer less than six months.
- address is a post office box or mail drop.
- does not have a telephone

- does not have a telephone
- listed number is a mobile/cellular phone
- is difficult to contact.
- frequently changes address and/or phone number.
- place of contact is a hotel, tavern, or other place which is neither his/her place of employment nor place of residence.
- handles all business in person, thus avoiding use of the mail.
- is unemployed.
- claim to be self-employed but is vague about the business and actual responsibilities.
- has recent or current marital and/or financial problems.
- has a temporary, recently issued, or out-of-state driver's license.
- driver's license has recently been suspended.
- recently called to confirm and/or increase coverage
- has an accumulation of parking tickets on the vehicle.
- is unusually aggressive and pressures for a quick settlement.
- offers inducement for quick settlement
- is very knowledgeable of claims process and insurance terminology
- income is not compatible with value of insured vehicle.
- claims expensive contents in vehicle at time of theft.
- is employed with another insurance company.
- wants a friend or relative to pick up the settlement check.
- is behind in loan payment on vehicle and/or other financial obligations.
- avoids meeting with investigators and/or claims adjusters.
- cancels scheduled appointments with claims adjusters for statements and/or examination under oath.

Indicators of Fraud Related To The Vehicle

Vehicle:

- was purchased for cash with no Bill of Sale or proof of ownership.
- is a new or late model with no lien holder.
- was very recently purchased
- was not seen for an extended period of time prior to the reported theft.
- was purchased out of state.
- has a history of mechanical problems.
- is a "gas guzzler."
- is customized, classic, and/or antique.
- displayed "For Sale" signs prior to theft.
- was recovered clinically/carefully stripped.
- is parked on the street although a garage is available.

- was recovered stripped, but insured wants to regain salvage, and repairs appear to be impractical.
- is recovered by the insured or a friend.
- purchase price was exceptionally high or low.
- was recovered with old or recent damage and coverage was high deductible or no collision coverage.
- coverage is only on a binder
- has an incorrect VIN (e.g., not originally manufactured, inconsistent with model).
- VIN is different than VIN appearing on title.
- VIN provided to police is incorrect.
- safety certification label is altered or missing.
- safety certification labels displays different VIN than is displayed on vehicle.
- has theft and/or salvage history.
- is recovered with no ignition or steering lock damage.
- is recovered with seized engine or blown transmission.
- was previously involved in a major collision.
- is late model with extremely high mileage (exception: taxi, policy, utility vehicles).
- is older with extremely low mileage (i.e., odometer rollover/rollback).
- is older or inexpensive model and insured indicates it was equipped with expensive accessories which cannot be substantiated with receipts.
- is recovered stripped, burned, or has severe collision damage within a short duration of time after loss allegedly occurred.
- leased vehicles with excessive mileage for which the insured would have been liable under the mileage limitation agreement.

Indicators of Fraud Related to Coverage

- loss occurs within one month of issue or expiration of policy
- loss occurs after cancellation notice was sent to the insured.
- insurance premium was paid in cash.
- coverage obtained via walk-in business to agent.
- coverage obtained from agent not located in close proximity to insured's residence or work place.
- coverage is for minimum liability with full comprehensive coverage on late model and/or expensive vehicle.
- coverage was recently increased.

Indicators of Fraud Related to Reporting
- police report has not been made by insured or has been delayed.
- no report or claim is made to insurance carrier within one week after theft.
- neighbors, friends and family are not aware of loss.
- license plate does not match vehicle and/or is not registered to insured.
- title is junk, salvage, out-of-state, photocopied, or duplicated.
- title history shows non-existent addresses.
- repair bills are consecutively numbered or dates show work accomplished on weekends or holidays.
- an individual, rather than a bank or financial institution, is named as lien holder.

Other General Indicators of Vehicle Theft Fraud
- vehicle is towed to isolated yard at owner's request.
- salvage yard or repair garage takes unusual interest in claim.
- information concerning prior owner is unavailable.
- prior owner cannot be located.
- vehicle is recovered totally burned after theft.
- fire damage is inconsistent with loss description.
- VINs were removed prior to fire.

Appendix D — Specimen Forms and Endorsements

CA 00 01 10 01	Business Auto Coverage Form, 135
CA DS 03 02 04	Business Auto Declarations, 146
CA 20 01 10 01	Lessor—Additional Insured and Loss Payee, 152
CA 99 03 07 97	Auto Medical Payments Coverage, 154
CA 99 10 09 02	Drive Other Car Coverage—Broadened Coverage for Named Individuals, 156
CA 99 16 12 93	Hired Autos Specified As Covered Autos You Own, 158
CA 99 17 10 01	Individual Named Insured, 159
CA 01 21 02 99	Limited Mexico Coverage, 161
CA 20 48 02 99	Designated Insured, 162
CA 20 54 10 01	Employee Hired Autos, 163
CA 20 71 10 01	Auto Loan/Lease Gap Coverage, 164
CA 00 51 12 04	Changes In Coverage Forms—Mobile Equipment Subject To Motor Vehicle Insurance Laws, 165
CA 20 15 12 04	Mobile Equipment, 166
IL 00 17 11 98	Common Policy Conditions, 168

COMMERCIAL AUTO
CA 00 01 10 01

BUSINESS AUTO COVERAGE FORM

Various provisions in this policy restrict coverage. Read the entire policy carefully to determine rights, duties and what is and is not covered.

Throughout this policy the words "you" and "your" refer to the Named Insured shown in the Declarations. The words "we", "us" and "our" refer to the Company providing this insurance.

Other words and phrases that appear in quotation marks have special meaning. Refer to Section **V** – Definitions.

SECTION I – COVERED AUTOS

Item Two of the Declarations shows the "autos" that are covered "autos" for each of your coverages. The following numerical symbols describe the "autos" that may be covered "autos". The symbols entered next to a coverage on the Declarations designate the only "autos" that are covered "autos".

A. Description Of Covered Auto Designation Symbols

Symbol	Description Of Covered Auto Designation Symbols	
1	Any "Auto"	
2	Owned "Autos" Only	Only those "autos" you own (and for Liability Coverage any "trailers" you don't own while attached to power units you own). This includes those "autos" you acquire ownership of after the policy begins.
3	Owned Private Passenger "Autos" Only	Only the private passenger "autos" you own. This includes those private passenger "autos" you acquire ownership of after the policy begins.
4	Owned "Autos" Other Than Private Passenger "Autos" Only	Only those "autos" you own that are not of the private passenger type (and for Liability Coverage any "trailers" you don't own while attached to power units you own). This includes those "autos" not of the private passenger type you acquire ownership of after the policy begins.
5	Owned "Autos" Subject To No-Fault	Only those "autos" you own that are required to have No-Fault benefits in the state where they are licensed or principally garaged. This includes those "autos" you acquire ownership of after the policy begins provided they are required to have No-Fault benefits in the state where they are licensed or principally garaged.
6	Owned "Autos" Subject To A Compulsory Uninsured Motorists Law	Only those "autos" you own that because of the law in the state where they are licensed or principally garaged are required to have and cannot reject Uninsured Motorists Coverage. This includes those "autos" you acquire ownership of after the policy begins provided they are subject to the same state uninsured motorists requirement.
7	Specifically Described "Autos"	Only those "autos" described in Item Three of the Declarations for which a premium charge is shown (and for Liability Coverage any "trailers" you don't own while attached to any power unit described in Item Three).
8	Hired "Autos" Only	Only those "autos" you lease, hire, rent or borrow. This does not include any "auto" you lease, hire, rent, or borrow from any of your "employees", partners (if you are a partnership), members (if you are a limited liability company) or members of their households.
9	Nonowned "Autos" Only	Only those "autos" you do not own, lease, hire, rent or borrow that are used in connection with your business. This includes "autos" owned by your "employees", partners (if you are a partnership), members (if you are a limited liability company), or members of their households but only while used in your business or your personal affairs.

B. **Owned Autos You Acquire After The Policy Begins**

1. If Symbols **1, 2, 3, 4, 5** or **6** are entered next to a coverage in Item Two of the Declarations, then you have coverage for "autos" that you acquire of the type described for the remainder of the policy period.

2. But, if Symbol **7** is entered next to a coverage in Item Two of the Declarations, an "auto" you acquire will be a covered "auto" for that coverage only if:

   a. We already cover all "autos" that you own for that coverage or it replaces an "auto" you previously owned that had that coverage; and

   b. You tell us within 30 days after you acquire it that you want us to cover it for that coverage.

C. **Certain Trailers, Mobile Equipment And Temporary Substitute Autos**

If Liability Coverage is provided by this Coverage Form, the following types of vehicles are also covered "autos" for Liability Coverage:

1. "Trailers" with a load capacity of 2,000 pounds or less designed primarily for travel on public roads.

2. "Mobile equipment" while being carried or towed by a covered "auto".

3. Any "auto" you do not own while used with the permission of its owner as a temporary substitute for a covered "auto" you own that is out of service because of its:

   a. Breakdown;
   b. Repair;
   c. Servicing;
   d. "Loss"; or
   e. Destruction.

SECTION II – LIABILITY COVERAGE

A. **Coverage**

We will pay all sums an "insured" legally must pay as damages because of "bodily injury" or "property damage" to which this insurance applies, caused by an "accident" and resulting from the ownership, maintenance or use of a covered "auto".

We will also pay all sums an "insured" legally must pay as a "covered pollution cost or expense" to which this insurance applies, caused by an "accident" and resulting from the ownership, maintenance or use of covered "autos". However, we will only pay for the "covered pollution cost or expense" if there is either "bodily injury" or "property damage" to which this insurance applies that is caused by the same "accident".

We have the right and duty to defend any "insured" against a "suit" asking for such damages or a "covered pollution cost or expense". However, we have no duty to defend any "insured" against a "suit" seeking damages for "bodily injury" or "property damage" or a "covered pollution cost or expense" to which this insurance does not apply. We may investigate and settle any claim or "suit" as we consider appropriate. Our duty to defend or settle ends when the Liability Coverage Limit of Insurance has been exhausted by payment of judgments or settlements.

1. **Who Is An Insured**

   The following are "insureds":

   a. You for any covered "auto".

   b. Anyone else while using with your permission a covered "auto" you own, hire or borrow except:

      (1) The owner or anyone else from whom you hire or borrow a covered "auto". This exception does not apply if the covered "auto" is a "trailer" connected to a covered "auto" you own.

      (2) Your "employee" if the covered "auto" is owned by that "employee" or a member of his or her household.

      (3) Someone using a covered "auto" while he or she is working in a business of selling, servicing, repairing, parking or storing "autos" unless that business is yours.

      (4) Anyone other than your "employees", partners (if you are a partnership), members (if you are a limited liability company), or a lessee or borrower or any of their "employees", while moving property to or from a covered "auto".

      (5) A partner (if you are a partnership), or a member (if you are a limited liability company) for a covered "auto" owned by him or her or a member of his or her household.

c. Anyone liable for the conduct of an "insured" described above but only to the extent of that liability.

2. **Coverage Extensions**

   a. **Supplementary Payments**

   In addition to the Limit of Insurance, we will pay for the "insured":

   (1) All expenses we incur.

   (2) Up to $2,000 for cost of bail bonds (including bonds for related traffic law violations) required because of an "accident" we cover. We do not have to furnish these bonds.

   (3) The cost of bonds to release attachments in any "suit" against the "insured" we defend, but only for bond amounts within our Limit of Insurance.

   (4) All reasonable expenses incurred by the "insured" at our request, including actual loss of earnings up to $250 a day because of time off from work.

   (5) All costs taxed against the "insured" in any "suit" against the "insured" we defend.

   (6) All interest on the full amount of any judgment that accrues after entry of the judgment in any "suit" against the "insured" we defend, but our duty to pay interest ends when we have paid, offered to pay or deposited in court the part of the judgment that is within our Limit of Insurance.

   b. **Out-Of-State Coverage Extensions**

   While a covered "auto" is away from the state where it is licensed we will:

   (1) Increase the Limit of Insurance for Liability Coverage to meet the limits specified by a compulsory or financial responsibility law of the jurisdiction where the covered "auto" is being used. This extension does not apply to the limit or limits specified by any law governing motor carriers of passengers or property.

   (2) Provide the minimum amounts and types of other coverages, such as no-fault, required of out-of-state vehicles by the jurisdiction where the covered "auto" is being used.

   We will not pay anyone more than once for the same elements of loss because of these extensions.

B. **Exclusions**

This insurance does not apply to any of the following:

1. **Expected Or Intended Injury**

   "Bodily injury" or "property damage" expected or intended from the standpoint of the "insured".

2. **Contractual**

   Liability assumed under any contract or agreement.

   But this exclusion does not apply to liability for damages:

   a. Assumed in a contract or agreement that is an "insured contract" provided the "bodily injury" or "property damage" occurs subsequent to the execution of the contract or agreement; or

   b. That the "insured" would have in the absence of the contract or agreement.

3. **Workers' Compensation**

   Any obligation for which the "insured" or the "insured's" insurer may be held liable under any workers' compensation, disability benefits or unemployment compensation law or any similar law.

4. **Employee Indemnification And Employer's Liability**

   "Bodily injury" to:

   a. An "employee" of the "insured" arising out of and in the course of:

   (1) Employment by the "insured"; or

   (2) Performing the duties related to the conduct of the "insured's" business; or

   b. The spouse, child, parent, brother or sister of that "employee" as a consequence of Paragraph **a.** above.

   This exclusion applies:

   (1) Whether the "insured" may be liable as an employer or in any other capacity; and

   (2) To any obligation to share damages with or repay someone else who must pay damages because of the injury.

   But this exclusion does not apply to "bodily injury" to domestic "employees" not entitled to workers' compensation benefits or to liability assumed by the "insured" under an "insured contract". For the purposes of the Coverage Form, a domestic "employee" is a person engaged in household or domestic work performed principally in connection with a residence premises.

5. Fellow Employee

"Bodily injury" to any fellow "employee" of the "insured" arising out of and in the course of the fellow "employee's" employment or while performing duties related to the conduct of your business.

6. Care, Custody Or Control

"Property damage" to or "covered pollution cost or expense" involving property owned or transported by the "insured" or in the "insured's" care, custody or control. But this exclusion does not apply to liability assumed under a sidetrack agreement.

7. Handling Of Property

"Bodily injury" or "property damage" resulting from the handling of property:

a. Before it is moved from the place where it is accepted by the "insured" for movement into or onto the covered "auto"; or

b. After it is moved from the covered "auto" to the place where it is finally delivered by the "insured".

8. Movement Of Property By Mechanical Device

"Bodily injury" or "property damage" resulting from the movement of property by a mechanical device (other than a hand truck) unless the device is attached to the covered "auto".

9. Operations

"Bodily injury" or "property damage" arising out of the operation of any equipment listed in Paragraphs **6.b.** and **6.c.** of the definition of "mobile equipment".

10. Completed Operations

"Bodily injury" or "property damage" arising out of your work after that work has been completed or abandoned.

In this exclusion, your work means:

a. Work or operations performed by you or on your behalf; and

b. Materials, parts or equipment furnished in connection with such work or operations.

Your work includes warranties or representations made at any time with respect to the fitness, quality, durability or performance of any of the items included in Paragraphs **a.** or **b.** above.

Your work will be deemed completed at the earliest of the following times:

(1) When all of the work called for in your contract has been completed.

(2) When all of the work to be done at the site has been completed if your contract calls for work at more than one site.

(3) When that part of the work done at a job site has been put to its intended use by any person or organization other than another contractor or subcontractor working on the same project.

Work that may need service, maintenance, correction, repair or replacement, but which is otherwise complete, will be treated as completed.

11. Pollution

"Bodily injury" or "property damage" arising out of the actual, alleged or threatened discharge, dispersal, seepage, migration, release or escape of "pollutants":

a. That are, or that are contained in any property that is:

(1) Being transported or towed by, handled, or handled for movement into, onto or from, the covered "auto";

(2) Otherwise in the course of transit by or on behalf of the "insured"; or

(3) Being stored, disposed of, treated or processed in or upon the covered "auto";

b. Before the "pollutants" or any property in which the "pollutants" are contained are moved from the place where they are accepted by the "insured" for movement into or onto the covered "auto"; or

c. After the "pollutants" or any property in which the "pollutants" are contained are moved from the covered "auto" to the place where they are finally delivered, disposed of or abandoned by the "insured".

Paragraph **a.** above does not apply to fuels, lubricants, fluids, exhaust gases or other similar "pollutants" that are needed for or result from the normal electrical, hydraulic or mechanical functioning of the covered "auto" or its parts, if:

(1) The "pollutants" escape, seep, migrate, or are discharged, dispersed or released directly from an "auto" part designed by its manufacturer to hold, store, receive or dispose of such "pollutants"; and

(2) The "bodily injury", "property damage" or "covered pollution cost or expense" does not arise out of the operation of any equipment listed in Paragraphs **6.b.** and **6.c.** of the definition of "mobile equipment".

Paragraphs **b.** and **c.** above of this exclusion do not apply to "accidents" that occur away from premises owned by or rented to an "insured" with respect to "pollutants" not in or upon a covered "auto" if:

(1) The "pollutants" or any property in which the "pollutants" are contained are upset, overturned or damaged as a result of the maintenance or use of a covered "auto"; and

(2) The discharge, dispersal, seepage, migration, release or escape of the "pollutants" is caused directly by such upset, overturn or damage.

12. War

"Bodily injury" or "property damage" due to war, whether or not declared, or any act or condition incident to war. War includes civil war, insurrection, rebellion or revolution. This exclusion applies only to liability assumed under a contract or agreement.

13. Racing

Covered "autos" while used in any professional or organized racing or demolition contest or stunting activity, or while practicing for such contest or activity. This insurance also does not apply while that covered "auto" is being prepared for such a contest or activity.

C. Limit Of Insurance

Regardless of the number of covered "autos", "insureds", premiums paid, claims made or vehicles involved in the "accident", the most we will pay for the total of all damages and "covered pollution cost or expense" combined, resulting from any one "accident" is the Limit of Insurance for Liability Coverage shown in the Declarations.

All "bodily injury", "property damage" and "covered pollution cost or expense" resulting from continuous or repeated exposure to substantially the same conditions will be considered as resulting from one "accident".

No one will be entitled to receive duplicate payments for the same elements of "loss" under this Coverage Form and any Medical Payments Coverage Endorsement, Uninsured Motorists Coverage Endorsement or Underinsured Motorists Coverage Endorsement attached to this Coverage Part.

SECTION III – PHYSICAL DAMAGE COVERAGE

A. Coverage

1. We will pay for "loss" to a covered "auto" or its equipment under:

    a. Comprehensive Coverage

    From any cause except:

    (1) The covered "auto's" collision with another object; or

    (2) The covered "auto's" overturn.

    b. Specified Causes Of Loss Coverage

    Caused by:

    (1) Fire, lightning or explosion;

    (2) Theft;

    (3) Windstorm, hail or earthquake;

    (4) Flood;

    (5) Mischief or vandalism; or

    (6) The sinking, burning, collision or derailment of any conveyance transporting the covered "auto".

    c. Collision Coverage

    Caused by:

    (1) The covered "auto's" collision with another object; or

    (2) The covered "auto's" overturn.

2. **Towing**

    We will pay up to the limit shown in the Declarations for towing and labor costs incurred each time a covered "auto" of the private passenger type is disabled. However, the labor must be performed at the place of disablement.

3. **Glass Breakage – Hitting A Bird Or Animal – Falling Objects Or Missiles**

    If you carry Comprehensive Coverage for the damaged covered "auto", we will pay for the following under Comprehensive Coverage:

    a. Glass breakage;

    b. "Loss" caused by hitting a bird or animal; and

    c. "Loss" caused by falling objects or missiles.

    However, you have the option of having glass breakage caused by a covered "auto's" collision or overturn considered a "loss" under Collision Coverage.

4. Coverage Extensions

a. Transportation Expenses

We will pay up to $20 per day to a maximum of $600 for temporary transportation expense incurred by you because of the total theft of a covered "auto" of the private passenger type. We will pay only for those covered "autos" for which you carry either Comprehensive or Specified Causes of Loss Coverage. We will pay for temporary transportation expenses incurred during the period beginning 48 hours after the theft and ending, regardless of the policy's expiration, when the covered "auto" is returned to use or we pay for its "loss".

b. Loss Of Use Expenses

For Hired Auto Physical Damage, we will pay expenses for which an "insured" becomes legally responsible to pay for loss of use of a vehicle rented or hired without a driver, under a written rental contract or agreement. We will pay for loss of use expenses if caused by:

(1) Other than collision only if the Declarations indicate that Comprehensive Coverage is provided for any covered "auto";

(2) Specified Causes Of Loss only if the Declarations indicate that Specified Causes Of Loss Coverage is provided for any covered "auto"; or

(3) Collision only if the Declarations indicate that Collision Coverage is provided for any covered "auto".

However, the most we will pay for any expenses for loss of use is $20 per day, to a maximum of $600.

B. Exclusions

1. We will not pay for "loss" caused by or resulting from any of the following. Such "loss" is excluded regardless of any other cause or event that contributes concurrently or in any sequence to the "loss".

   ### a. Nuclear Hazard

   (1) The explosion of any weapon employing atomic fission or fusion; or

   (2) Nuclear reaction or radiation, or radioactive contamination, however caused.

   ### b. War Or Military Action

   (1) War, including undeclared or civil war;

   (2) Warlike action by a military force, including action in hindering or defending against an actual or expected attack, by any government, sovereign or other authority using military personnel or other agents; or

   (3) Insurrection, rebellion, revolution, usurped power or action taken by governmental authority in hindering or defending against any of these.

2. We will not pay for "loss" to any covered "auto" while used in any professional or organized racing or demolition contest or stunting activity, or while practicing for such contest or activity. We will also not pay for "loss" to any covered "auto" while that covered "auto" is being prepared for such a contest or activity.

3. We will not pay for "loss" caused by or resulting from any of the following unless caused by other "loss" that is covered by this insurance:

   a. Wear and tear, freezing, mechanical or electrical breakdown.

   b. Blowouts, punctures or other road damage to tires.

4. We will not pay for "loss" to any of the following:

   a. Tapes, records, discs or other similar audio, visual or data electronic devices designed for use with audio, visual or data electronic equipment.

   b. Any device designed or used to detect speed measuring equipment such as radar or laser detectors and any jamming apparatus intended to elude or disrupt speed measurement equipment.

   c. Any electronic equipment, without regard to whether this equipment is permanently installed, that receives or transmits audio, visual or data signals and that is not designed solely for the reproduction of sound.

   d. Any accessories used with the electronic equipment described in Paragraph **c.** above.

Exclusions **4.c.** and **4.d.** do not apply to:

a. Equipment designed solely for the reproduction of sound and accessories used with such equipment, provided such equipment is permanently installed in the covered "auto" at the time of the "loss" or such equipment is removable from a housing unit which is permanently installed in the covered "auto" at the time of the "loss", and such equipment is designed to be solely operated by use of the power from the "auto's" electrical system, in or upon the covered "auto"; or

b. Any other electronic equipment that is:

(1) Necessary for the normal operation of the covered "auto" or the monitoring of the covered "auto's" operating system; or

(2) An integral part of the same unit housing any sound reproducing equipment described in **a.** above and permanently installed in the opening of the dash or console of the covered "auto" normally used by the manufacturer for installation of a radio.

5. We will not pay for "loss" to a covered "auto" due to "diminution in value".

C. Limit Of Insurance

1. The most we will pay for "loss" in any one "accident" is the lesser of:

    a. The actual cash value of the damaged or stolen property as of the time of the "loss"; or

    b. The cost of repairing or replacing the damaged or stolen property with other property of like kind and quality.

2. An adjustment for depreciation and physical condition will be made in determining actual cash value in the event of a total "loss".

3. If a repair or replacement results in better than like kind or quality, we will not pay for the amount of the betterment.

D. Deductible

For each covered "auto", our obligation to pay for, repair, return or replace damaged or stolen property will be reduced by the applicable deductible shown in the Declarations. Any Comprehensive Coverage deductible shown in the Declarations does not apply to "loss" caused by fire or lightning.

SECTION IV – BUSINESS AUTO CONDITIONS

The following conditions apply in addition to the Common Policy Conditions:

A. Loss Conditions

1. **Appraisal For Physical Damage Loss**

    If you and we disagree on the amount of "loss", either may demand an appraisal of the "loss". In this event, each party will select a competent appraiser. The two appraisers will select a competent and impartial umpire. The appraisers will state separately the actual cash value and amount of "loss". If they fail to agree, they will submit their differences to the umpire. A decision agreed to by any two will be binding. Each party will:

    a. Pay its chosen appraiser; and

    b. Bear the other expenses of the appraisal and umpire equally.

    If we submit to an appraisal, we will still retain our right to deny the claim.

2. **Duties In The Event Of Accident, Claim, Suit Or Loss**

    We have no duty to provide coverage under this policy unless there has been full compliance with the following duties:

    a. In the event of "accident", claim, "suit" or "loss", you must give us or our authorized representative prompt notice of the "accident" or "loss". Include:

    (1) How, when and where the "accident" or "loss" occurred;

    (2) The "insured's" name and address; and

    (3) To the extent possible, the names and addresses of any injured persons and witnesses.

    b. Additionally, you and any other involved "insured" must:

    (1) Assume no obligation, make no payment or incur no expense without our consent, except at the "insured's" own cost.

    (2) Immediately send us copies of any request, demand, order, notice, summons or legal paper received concerning the claim or "suit".

    (3) Cooperate with us in the investigation or settlement of the claim or defense against the "suit".

    (4) Authorize us to obtain medical records or other pertinent information.

(5) Submit to examination, at our expense, by physicians of our choice, as often as we reasonably require.

c. If there is "loss" to a covered "auto" or its equipment you must also do the following:

(1) Promptly notify the police if the covered "auto" or any of its equipment is stolen.

(2) Take all reasonable steps to protect the covered "auto" from further damage. Also keep a record of your expenses for consideration in the settlement of the claim.

(3) Permit us to inspect the covered "auto" and records proving the "loss" before its repair or disposition.

(4) Agree to examinations under oath at our request and give us a signed statement of your answers.

3. **Legal Action Against Us**

No one may bring a legal action against us under this Coverage Form until:

a. There has been full compliance with all the terms of this Coverage Form; and

b. Under Liability Coverage, we agree in writing that the "insured" has an obligation to pay or until the amount of that obligation has finally been determined by judgment after trial. No one has the right under this policy to bring us into an action to determine the "insured's" liability.

4. **Loss Payment – Physical Damage Coverages**

At our option we may:

a. Pay for, repair or replace damaged or stolen property;

b. Return the stolen property, at our expense. We will pay for any damage that results to the "auto" from the theft; or

c. Take all or any part of the damaged or stolen property at an agreed or appraised value.

If we pay for the "loss", our payment will include the applicable sales tax for the damaged or stolen property.

5. **Transfer Of Rights Of Recovery Against Others To Us**

If any person or organization to or for whom we make payment under this Coverage Form has rights to recover damages from another, those rights are transferred to us. That person or organization must do everything necessary to secure our rights and must do nothing after "accident" or "loss" to impair them.

B. **General Conditions**

1. **Bankruptcy**

Bankruptcy or insolvency of the "insured" or the "insured's" estate will not relieve us of any obligations under this Coverage Form.

2. **Concealment, Misrepresentation Or Fraud**

This Coverage Form is void in any case of fraud by you at any time as it relates to this Coverage Form. It is also void if you or any other "insured", at any time, intentionally conceal or misrepresent a material fact concerning:

a. This Coverage Form;

b. The covered "auto";

c. Your interest in the covered "auto"; or

d. A claim under this Coverage Form.

3. **Liberalization**

If we revise this Coverage Form to provide more coverage without additional premium charge, your policy will automatically provide the additional coverage as of the day the revision is effective in your state.

4. **No Benefit To Bailee – Physical Damage Coverages**

We will not recognize any assignment or grant any coverage for the benefit of any person or organization holding, storing or transporting property for a fee regardless of any other provision of this Coverage Form.

5. **Other Insurance**

a. For any covered "auto" you own, this Coverage Form provides primary insurance. For any covered "auto" you don't own, the insurance provided by this Coverage Form is excess over any other collectible insurance. However, while a covered "auto" which is a "trailer" is connected to another vehicle, the Liability Coverage this Coverage Form provides for the "trailer" is:

(1) Excess while it is connected to a motor vehicle you do not own.

(2) Primary while it is connected to a covered "auto" you own.

b. For Hired Auto Physical Damage Coverage, any covered "auto" you lease, hire, rent or borrow is deemed to be a covered "auto" you own. However, any "auto" that is leased, hired, rented or borrowed with a driver is not a covered "auto".

c. Regardless of the provisions of Paragraph a. above, this Coverage Form's Liability Coverage is primary for any liability assumed under an "insured contract".

d. When this Coverage Form and any other Coverage Form or policy covers on the same basis, either excess or primary, we will pay only our share. Our share is the proportion that the Limit of Insurance of our Coverage Form bears to the total of the limits of all the Coverage Forms and policies covering on the same basis.

6. **Premium Audit**

   a. The estimated premium for this Coverage Form is based on the exposures you told us you would have when this policy began. We will compute the final premium due when we determine your actual exposures. The estimated total premium will be credited against the final premium due and the first Named Insured will be billed for the balance, if any. The due date for the final premium or retrospective premium is the date shown as the due date on the bill. If the estimated total premium exceeds the final premium due, the first Named Insured will get a refund.

   b. If this policy is issued for more than one year, the premium for this Coverage Form will be computed annually based on our rates or premiums in effect at the beginning of each year of the policy.

7. **Policy Period, Coverage Territory**

   Under this Coverage Form, we cover "accidents" and "losses" occurring:

   a. During the policy period shown in the Declarations; and

   b. Within the coverage territory.

   The coverage territory is:

   a. The United States of America;

   b. The territories and possessions of the United States of America;

   c. Puerto Rico;

   d. Canada; and

   e. Anywhere in the world if:

      (1) A covered "auto" of the private passenger type is leased, hired, rented or borrowed without a driver for a period of 30 days or less; and

      (2) The "insured's" responsibility to pay damages is determined in a "suit" on the merits, in the United States of America, the territories and possessions of the United States of America, Puerto Rico, or Canada or in a settlement we agree to.

We also cover "loss" to, or "accidents" involving, a covered "auto" while being transported between any of these places.

8. **Two Or More Coverage Forms Or Policies Issued By Us**

   If this Coverage Form and any other Coverage Form or policy issued to you by us or any company affiliated with us apply to the same "accident", the aggregate maximum Limit of Insurance under all the Coverage Forms or policies shall not exceed the highest applicable Limit of Insurance under any one Coverage Form or policy. This condition does not apply to any Coverage Form or policy issued by us or an affiliated company specifically to apply as excess insurance over this Coverage Form.

SECTION V – DEFINITIONS

A. "Accident" includes continuous or repeated exposure to the same conditions resulting in "bodily injury" or "property damage".

B. "Auto" means a land motor vehicle, "trailer" or semitrailer designed for travel on public roads but does not include "mobile equipment".

C. "Bodily injury" means bodily injury, sickness or disease sustained by a person including death resulting from any of these.

D. "Covered pollution cost or expense" means any cost or expense arising out of:

   1. Any request, demand, order or statutory or regulatory requirement; or

   2. Any claim or "suit" by or on behalf of a governmental authority demanding

   that the "insured" or others test for, monitor, clean up, remove, contain, treat, detoxify or neutralize, or in any way respond to, or assess the effects of "pollutants".

   "Covered pollution cost or expense" does not include any cost or expense arising out of the actual, alleged or threatened discharge, dispersal, seepage, migration, release or escape of "pollutants":

   a. That are, or that are contained in any property that is:

      (1) Being transported or towed by, handled, or handled for movement into, onto or from the covered "auto";

      (2) Otherwise in the course of transit by or on behalf of the "insured";

      (3) Being stored, disposed of, treated or processed in or upon the covered "auto",

b. Before the "pollutants" or any property in which the "pollutants" are contained are moved from the place where they are accepted by the "insured" for movement into or onto the covered "auto"; or

c. After the "pollutants" or any property in which the "pollutants" are contained are moved from the covered "auto" to the place where they are finally delivered, disposed of or abandoned by the "insured".

Paragraph **a.** above does not apply to fuels, lubricants, fluids, exhaust gases or other similar "pollutants" that are needed for or result from the normal electrical, hydraulic or mechanical functioning of the covered "auto" or its parts, if:

(1) The "pollutants" escape, seep, migrate, or are discharged, dispersed or released directly from an "auto" part designed by its manufacturer to hold, store, receive or dispose of such "pollutants"; and

(2) The "bodily injury", "property damage" or "covered pollution cost or expense" does not arise out of the operation of any equipment listed in Paragraphs **6.b.** or **6.c.** of the definition of "mobile equipment".

Paragraphs **b.** and **c.** above do not apply to "accidents" that occur away from premises owned by or rented to an "insured" with respect to "pollutants" not in or upon a covered "auto" if:

(1) The "pollutants" or any property in which the "pollutants" are contained are upset, overturned or damaged as a result of the maintenance or use of a covered "auto"; and

(2) The discharge, dispersal, seepage, migration, release or escape of the "pollutants" is caused directly by such upset, overturn or damage.

E. "Diminution in value" means the actual or perceived loss in market value or resale value which results from a direct and accidental "loss".

F. "Employee" includes a "leased worker". "Employee" does not include a "temporary worker".

G. "Insured" means any person or organization qualifying as an insured in the Who Is An Insured provision of the applicable coverage. Except with respect to the Limit of Insurance, the coverage afforded applies separately to each insured who is seeking coverage or against whom a claim or "suit" is brought.

H. "Insured contract" means:

1. A lease of premises;

2. A sidetrack agreement;

3. Any easement or license agreement, except in connection with construction or demolition operations on or within 50 feet of a railroad;

4. An obligation, as required by ordinance, to indemnify a municipality, except in connection with work for a municipality;

5. That part of any other contract or agreement pertaining to your business (including an indemnification of a municipality in connection with work performed for a municipality) under which you assume the tort liability of another to pay for "bodily injury" or "property damage" to a third party or organization. Tort liability means a liability that would be imposed by law in the absence of any contract or agreement;

6. That part of any contract or agreement entered into, as part of your business, pertaining to the rental or lease, by you or any of your "employees", of any "auto". However, such contract or agreement shall not be considered an "insured contract" to the extent that it obligates you or any of your "employees" to pay for "property damage" to any "auto" rented or leased by you or any of your "employees".

An "insured contract" does not include that part of any contract or agreement:

a. That indemnifies a railroad for "bodily injury" or "property damage" arising out of construction or demolition operations, within 50 feet of any railroad property and affecting any railroad bridge or trestle, tracks, roadbeds, tunnel, underpass or crossing; or

b. That pertains to the loan, lease or rental of an "auto" to you or any of your "employees", if the "auto" is loaned, leased or rented with a driver; or

c. That holds a person or organization engaged in the business of transporting property by "auto" for hire harmless for your use of a covered "auto" over a route or territory that person or organization is authorized to serve by public authority.

I. "Leased worker" means a person leased to you by a labor leasing firm under an agreement between you and the labor leasing firm, to perform duties related to the conduct of your business. "Leased worker" does not include a "temporary worker".

J. "Loss" means direct and accidental loss or damage.

K. "Mobile equipment" means any of the following types of land vehicles, including any attached machinery or equipment:
   1. Bulldozers, farm machinery, forklifts and other vehicles designed for use principally off public roads;
   2. Vehicles maintained for use solely on or next to premises you own or rent;
   3. Vehicles that travel on crawler treads;
   4. Vehicles, whether self-propelled or not, maintained primarily to provide mobility to permanently mounted:
      a. Power cranes, shovels, loaders, diggers or drills; or
      b. Road construction or resurfacing equipment such as graders, scrapers or rollers.
   5. Vehicles not described in Paragraphs **1.**, **2.**, **3.**, or **4.** above that are not self-propelled and are maintained primarily to provide mobility to permanently attached equipment of the following types:
      a. Air compressors, pumps and generators, including spraying, welding, building cleaning, geophysical exploration, lighting and well servicing equipment; or
      b. Cherry pickers and similar devices used to raise or lower workers.
   6. Vehicles not described in Paragraphs **1.**, **2.**, **3.** or **4.** above maintained primarily for purposes other than the transportation of persons or cargo. However, self-propelled vehicles with the following types of permanently attached equipment are not "mobile equipment" but will be considered "autos":
      a. Equipment designed primarily for:
         (1) Snow removal;
         (2) Road maintenance, but not construction or resurfacing; or
         (3) Street cleaning;
      b. Cherry pickers and similar devices mounted on automobile or truck chassis and used to raise or lower workers; and
      c. Air compressors, pumps and generators, including spraying, welding, building cleaning, geophysical exploration, lighting or well servicing equipment.

L. "Pollutants" means any solid, liquid, gaseous or thermal irritant or contaminant, including smoke, vapor, soot, fumes, acids, alkalis, chemicals and waste. Waste includes materials to be recycled, reconditioned or reclaimed.

M. "Property damage" means damage to or loss of use of tangible property.

N. "Suit" means a civil proceeding in which:
   1. Damages because of "bodily injury" or "property damage"; or
   2. A "covered pollution cost or expense",
   to which this insurance applies, are alleged.
   "Suit" includes:
      a. An arbitration proceeding in which such damages or "covered pollution costs or expenses" are claimed and to which the "insured" must submit or does submit with our consent; or
      b. Any other alternative dispute resolution proceeding in which such damages or "covered pollution costs or expenses" are claimed and to which the insured submits with our consent.

O. "Temporary worker" means a person who is furnished to you to substitute for a permanent "employee" on leave or to meet seasonal or short-term workload conditions.

P. "Trailer" includes semitrailer.

146   BUSINESS AUTO

POLICY NUMBER: COMMERCIAL AUTO
                                                        CA DS 03 02 04

BUSINESS AUTO DECLARATIONS

COMPANY NAME AREA	PRODUCER NAME AREA

ITEM ONE
NAMED INSURED:
MAILING ADDRESS:
POLICY PERIOD: From: to: at 12:01 A.M. Standard Time at your mailing address shown above.

PREVIOUS POLICY NUMBER:

FORM OF BUSINESS:
☐ CORPORATION   ☐ LIMITED LIABILITY COMPANY   ☐ INDIVIDUAL
☐ PARTNERSHIP   ☐ OTHER:

IN RETURN FOR THE PAYMENT OF THE PREMIUM, AND SUBJECT TO ALL THE TERMS OF THIS POLICY, WE AGREE WITH YOU TO PROVIDE THE INSURANCE AS STATED IN THIS POLICY.

PREMIUM FOR ENDORSEMENTS	$
*ESTIMATED TOTAL PREMIUM	$

*This policy may be subject to final audit.

Premium shown is payable: $ at inception.
AUDIT PERIOD (IF APPLICABLE) ☐ ANNUALLY   ☐ SEMI-ANNUALLY   ☐ QUARTERLY   ☐ MONTHLY

ENDORSEMENTS ATTACHED TO THIS POLICY:

   IL 00 17 – Common Policy Conditions (IL 01 46 in Washington)
   IL 00 21 – Broad Form Nuclear Exclusion (Not Applicable in New York)

Countersigned:	By:
(Date)	(Authorized Representative)

NOTE
OFFICERS' FACSIMILE SIGNATURES MAY BE INSERTED HERE, ON THE POLICY COVER OR ELSEWHERE AT THE COMPANY'S OPTION.

POLICY NUMBER:

ITEM TWO

SCHEDULE OF COVERAGES AND COVERED AUTOS

This policy provides only those coverages where a charge is shown in the premium column below. Each of these coverages will apply only to those "autos" shown as covered "autos". "Autos" are shown as covered "autos" for a particular coverage by the entry of one or more of the symbols from the Covered Autos Section of the Business Auto Coverage Form next to the name of the coverage.

COVERAGES	COVERED AUTOS (Entry of one or more of the symbols from the Covered Autos Section of the Business Auto Coverage Form shows which autos are covered autos.)	LIMIT THE MOST WE WILL PAY FOR ANY ONE ACCIDENT OR LOSS	PREMIUM
LIABILITY		$	$
PERSONAL INJURY PROTECTION (or equivalent No-fault Coverage)		SEPARATELY STATED IN EACH P.I.P. ENDORSEMENT MINUS $ DED.	$
ADDED PERSONAL INJURY PROTECTION (or equivalent added No-fault Coverage)		SEPARATELY STATED IN EACH ADDED P.I.P. ENDORSEMENT.	$
PROPERTY PROTECTION INSURANCE (Michigan only)		SEPARATELY STATED IN THE P.P.I. ENDORSEMENT MINUS $ DED. FOR EACH ACCIDENT.	$
AUTO MEDICAL PAYMENTS		$	$
MEDICAL EXPENSE AND INCOME LOSS BENEFITS (Virginia only)		SEPARATELY STATED IN EACH MEDICAL EXPENSE AND INCOME LOSS BENEFITS ENDORSEMENT.	$
UNINSURED MOTORISTS		$	$
UNDERINSURED MOTORISTS (When not included in Uninsured Motorists Coverage)		$	$
PHYSICAL DAMAGE COMPREHENSIVE COVERAGE		ACTUAL CASH VALUE OR COST OF REPAIR, WHICHEVER IS LESS, MINUS $ DED. FOR EACH COVERED AUTO, BUT NO DEDUCTIBLE APPLIES TO LOSS CAUSED BY FIRE OR LIGHTNING. See ITEM FOUR For Hired Or Borrowed "Autos".	$
PHYSICAL DAMAGE SPECIFIED CAUSES OF LOSS COVERAGE		ACTUAL CASH VALUE OR COST OF REPAIR, WHICHEVER IS LESS, MINUS $ DED. FOR EACH COVERED AUTO FOR LOSS CAUSED BY MISCHIEF OR VANDALISM. See ITEM FOUR For Hired Or Borrowed "Autos".	$
PHYSICAL DAMAGE COLLISION COVERAGE		ACTUAL CASH VALUE OR COST OF REPAIR, WHICHEVER IS LESS, MINUS $ DED. FOR EACH COVERED AUTO. See ITEM FOUR For Hired Or Borrowed "Autos".	$
PHYSICAL DAMAGE TOWING AND LABOR		$ For Each Disablement Of A Private Passenger "Auto".	$
			$
		PREMIUM FOR ENDORSEMENTS	$
		*ESTIMATED TOTAL PREMIUM	$

*This policy may be subject to final audit.

ITEM THREE

POLICY NUMBER:

SCHEDULE OF COVERED AUTOS YOU OWN

Covered Auto No.	DESCRIPTION Year, Model, Trade Name, Body Type Serial Number (S) Vehicle Identification Number (VIN)	PURCHASED		TERRITORY Town & State Where The Covered Auto Will Be Principally Garaged
		Original Cost New	Actual Cost & NEW (N) USED (U)	
1		$	$	
2		$	$	
3		$	$	
4		$	$	
5		$	$	

Covered Auto No.	CLASSIFICATION							EXCEPT For Towing, All Physical Damage Loss Is Payable To You And The Loss Payee Named Below As Interests May Appear At the Time Of The Loss.
	Radius Of Operation	Business Use s=service r=retail c=commercial	Size GVW, GCW Or Vehicle Seating Capacity	Age Group	Primary Rating Factor		Secondary Rating Factor	Code	
					Liab.	Phy. Dam.			
1									
2									
3									
4									
5									

Covered Auto No.	COVERAGES – PREMIUMS, LIMITS AND DEDUCTIBLES (Absence of a deductible or limit entry in any column below means that the limit or deductible entry in the corresponding ITEM TWO column applies instead.)							
	LIABILITY		PERSONAL INJURY PROTECTION		ADDED P.I.P.		PROPERTY PROTECTION (Michigan Only)	
	Limit	Premium	Limit Stated In Each P.I.P. End. Minus Deductible Shown Below	Premium	Limit Stated In Each Added P.I.P. End. Premium		Limit Stated In P.P.I. End. Minus Deductible Shown Below	Premium
1	$	$	$	$	$		$	$
2	$	$	$	$	$		$	$
3	$	$	$	$	$		$	$
4	$	$	$	$	$		$	$
5	$	$	$	$	$		$	$
Total Premium		$		$	$			$

CA DS 03 02 04 © ISO Properties, Inc., 2003

APPENDIX D - SPECIMEN FORMS   149

POLICY NUMBER:

ITEM THREE
SCHEDULE OF COVERED AUTOS YOU OWN (Cont'd)

Covered Auto No.	COVERAGES – PREMIUMS, LIMITS AND DEDUCTIBLES (Absence of a deductible or limit entry in any column below means that the limit or deductible entry in the corresponding ITEM TWO column applies instead.)			
	AUTO MEDICAL PAYMENTS		MEDICAL EXPENSE AND INCOME LOSS BENEFITS (Virginia Only)	
	Limit	Premium	Limit Stated In Each Medical Expense and Income Loss Endorsement For Each Person	Premium
1	$	$	$	$
2	$	$	$	$
3	$	$	$	$
4	$	$	$	$
5	$	$	$	$
Total Premium		$		$

Covered Auto No.	COVERAGES – PREMIUMS, LIMITS AND DEDUCTIBLES (Absence of a deductible or limit entry in any column below means that the limit or deductible entry in the corresponding ITEM TWO column applies instead.)							
	COMPREHENSIVE		SPECIFIED CAUSES OF LOSS		COLLISION		TOWING & LABOR	
	Limit Stated In ITEM TWO Minus Deductible Shown Below	Premium	Limit Stated In ITEM TWO Minus Deductible Shown Below	Premium	Limit Stated In ITEM TWO Minus Deductible Shown Below	Premium	Limit Per Disablement	Premium
1	$	$	$	$	$	$	$	$
2	$	$	$	$	$	$	$	$
3	$	$	$	$	$	$	$	$
4	$	$	$	$	$	$	$	$
5	$	$	$	$	$	$	$	$
Total Premium		$		$		$		$

ITEM FOUR
SCHEDULE OF HIRED OR BORROWED COVERED AUTO COVERAGE AND PREMIUMS

LIABILITY COVERAGE – RATING BASIS, COST OF HIRE				
STATE	ESTIMATED COST OF HIRE FOR EACH STATE	RATE PER EACH $100 COST OF HIRE	FACTOR (If Liability Coverage Is Primary)	PREMIUM
	$	$		$
			TOTAL PREMIUM	$

Cost of hire means the total amount you incur for the hire of "autos" you don't own (not including "autos" you borrow or rent from your partners or "employees" or their family members). Cost of hire does not include charges for services performed by motor carriers of property or passengers.

BUSINESS AUTO

PHYSICAL DAMAGE COVERAGE

POLICY NUMBER:

COVERAGES	LIMIT OF INSURANCE THE MOST WE WILL PAY DEDUCTIBLE	ESTIMATED ANNUAL COST OF HIRE	RATE PER EACH $100 ANNUAL COST OF HIRE	PREMIUM
COMPREHENSIVE	ACTUAL CASH VALUE OR COST OF REPAIR, WHICHEVER IS LESS, MINUS $ DED. FOR EACH COVERED AUTO, BUT NO DEDUCTIBLE APPLIES TO LOSS CAUSED BY FIRE OR LIGHTNING.	$	$	$
SPECIFIED CAUSES OF LOSS	ACTUAL CASH VALUE OR COST OF REPAIR, WHICHEVER IS LESS, MINUS $ DED. FOR EACH COVERED AUTO FOR LOSS CAUSED BY MISCHIEF OR VANDALISM.	$	$	$
COLLISION	ACTUAL CASH VALUE OR COST OF REPAIR, WHICHEVER IS LESS, MINUS $ DED. FOR EACH COVERED AUTO.	$	$	$
			TOTAL PREMIUM	$

ITEM FIVE
SCHEDULE FOR NON-OWNERSHIP LIABILITY

NAMED INSURED'S BUSINESS	RATING BASIS	NUMBER	PREMIUM
Other Than A Social Service Agency	Number Of Employees		$
	Number Of Partners		$
Social Service Agency	Number Of Employees		$
	Number Of Volunteers		$
		TOTAL	$

CA DS 03 02 04 © ISO Properties, Inc., 2003

APPENDIX D - SPECIMEN FORMS   151

POLICY NUMBER:

ITEM SIX

SCHEDULE FOR GROSS RECEIPTS OR MILEAGE BASIS – LIABILITY COVERAGE – PUBLIC AUTO OR LEASING RENTAL CONCERNS

ESTIMATED YEARLY	RATES				PREMIUMS			
☐ Gross Receipts ☐ Mileage	☐ Per $100 Of Gross Receipts ☐ Per Mile							
	LIABILITY	AUTO MEDICAL PAYMENTS	MEDICAL EXPENSE BENEFITS (VA. Only)	INCOME LOSS BENEFITS (VA. Only)	LIABILITY	AUTO MEDICAL PAYMENTS	MEDICAL EXPENSE BENEFITS (VA. Only)	INCOME LOSS BENEFITS (VA. Only)
	$	$	$	$	$	$	$	$
	$	$	$	$	$	$	$	$
	$	$	$	$	$	$	$	$
	$	$	$	$	$	$	$	$
				TOTAL PREMIUMS	$	$	$	$
				MINIMUM PREMIUMS	$	$	$	$

When used as a premium basis:

FOR PUBLIC AUTOS

Gross Receipts means the total amount to which you are entitled for transporting passengers, mail or merchandise during the policy period regardless of whether you or any other carrier originate the transportation. Gross Receipts does not include:

- A. Amounts you pay to railroads, steamship lines, airlines and other motor carriers operating under their own ICC or PUC permits.
- B. Advertising revenue.
- C. Taxes which you collect as a separate item and remit directly to a governmental division.
- D. C.O.D. collections for cost of mail or merchandise including collection fees.

Mileage means the total live and dead mileage of all revenue producing units operated during the policy period.

FOR RENTAL OR LEASING CONCERNS

Gross receipts means the total amount to which you are entitled for the leasing or rental of "autos" during the policy period and includes taxes except those taxes which you collect as a separate item and remit directly to a governmental division.

Mileage means the total of all live and dead mileage developed by all the "autos" you leased or rented to others during the policy period.

152 BUSINESS AUTO

POLICY NUMBER: COMMERCIAL AUTO
CA 20 01 10 01

THIS ENDORSEMENT CHANGES THE POLICY. PLEASE READ IT CAREFULLY.

LESSOR – ADDITIONAL INSURED AND LOSS PAYEE

This endorsement modifies insurance provided under the following:

BUSINESS AUTO COVERAGE FORM
BUSINESS AUTO PHYSICAL DAMAGE COVERAGE FORM
GARAGE COVERAGE FORM
MOTOR CARRIER COVERAGE FORM
TRUCKERS COVERAGE FORM

With respect to coverage provided by this endorsement, the provisions of the Coverage Form apply unless modified by the endorsement.

This endorsement changes the policy effective on the inception date of the policy unless another date is indicated below.

Endorsement Effective:	Countersigned By:
Named Insured:	(Authorized Representative)

SCHEDULE

| Insurance Company |
| Policy Number |
| Effective Date |
| Expiration Date |
| Named Insured
Address |
| Additional Insured (Lessor)
Address |
| Designation or Description of "Leased Autos" |

Coverages	Limit Of Insurance
Liability	$ Each "Accident"
Personal Injury Protection (or equivalent no-fault coverage)	$
Comprehensive	ACTUAL CASH VALUE OR COST OF REPAIR WHICHEVER IS LESS; MINUS: $ For Each Covered "Leased Auto"
Collision	ACTUAL CASH VALUE OR COST OF REPAIR WHICHEVER IS LESS; MINUS: $ For Each Covered "Leased Auto"
Specified Causes of Loss	ACTUAL CASH VALUE OR COST OF REPAIR WHICHEVER IS LESS; MINUS: $ For Each Covered "Leased Auto"

(If no entry appears above, information required to complete this endorsement will be shown in the Declarations as applicable to this endorsement.)

CA 20 01 10 01   © ISO Properties, Inc., 2000

A. Coverage

1. Any "leased auto" designated or described in the Schedule will be considered a covered "auto" you own and not a covered "auto" you hire or borrow. For a covered "auto" that is a "leased auto" **Who Is An Insured** is changed to include as an "insured" the lessor named in the Schedule.

2. The coverages provided under this endorsement apply to any "leased auto" described in the Schedule until the expiration date shown in the Schedule, or when the lessor or his or her agent takes possession of the "leased auto", whichever occurs first.

B. Loss Payable Clause

1. We will pay, as interest may appear, you and the lessor named in this endorsement for "loss" to a "leased auto".

2. The insurance covers the interest of the lessor unless the "loss" results from fraudulent acts or omissions on your part.

3. If we make any payment to the lessor, we will obtain his or her rights against any other party.

C. Cancellation

1. If we cancel the policy, we will mail notice to the lessor in accordance with the Cancellation Common Policy Condition.

2. If you cancel the policy, we will mail notice to the lessor.

3. Cancellation ends this agreement.

D.

The lessor is not liable for payment of your premiums.

E. Additional Definition

As used in this endorsement:

"Leased auto" means an "auto" leased or rented to you, including any substitute, replacement or extra "auto" needed to meet seasonal or other needs, under a leasing or rental agreement that requires you to provide direct primary insurance for the lessor.

154   BUSINESS AUTO

COMMERCIAL AUTO
CA 99 03 07 97

THIS ENDORSEMENT CHANGES THE POLICY. PLEASE READ IT CAREFULLY.

AUTO MEDICAL PAYMENTS COVERAGE

This endorsement modifies insurance provided under the following:

BUSINESS AUTO COVERAGE FORM
GARAGE COVERAGE FORM
MOTOR CARRIER COVERAGE FORM
TRUCKERS COVERAGE FORM

With respect to coverage provided by this endorsement, the provisions of the Coverage Form apply unless modified by the endorsement.

A. Coverage

We will pay reasonable expenses incurred for necessary medical and funeral services to or for an "insured" who sustains "bodily injury" caused by "accident". We will pay only those expenses incurred, for services rendered within three years from the date of the "accident".

B. Who Is An Insured

1. You while "occupying" or, while a pedestrian, when struck by any "auto".

2. If you are an individual, any "family member" while "occupying" or, while a pedestrian, when struck by any "auto".

3. Anyone else "occupying" a covered "auto" or a temporary substitute for a covered "auto". The covered "auto" must be out of service because of its breakdown, repair, servicing, loss or destruction.

C. Exclusions

This insurance does not apply to any of the following:

1. "Bodily injury" sustained by an "insured" while "occupying" a vehicle located for use as a premises.

2. "Bodily injury" sustained by you or any "family member" while "occupying" or struck by any vehicle (other than a covered "auto") owned by you or furnished or available for your regular use.

3. "Bodily injury" sustained by any "family member" while "occupying" or struck by any vehicle (other than a covered "auto") owned by or furnished or available for the regular use of any "family member".

4. "Bodily injury" to your "employee" arising out of and in the course of employment by you. However, we will cover "bodily injury" to your domestic "employees" if not entitled to workers' compensation benefits. For the purposes of this endorsement, a domestic "employee" is a person engaged in household or domestic work performed principally in connection with a residence premises.

5. "Bodily injury" to an "insured" while working in a business of selling, servicing, repairing or parking "autos" unless that business is yours.

6. "Bodily injury" caused by declared or undeclared war or insurrection or any of their consequences.

7. "Bodily injury" to anyone using a vehicle without a reasonable belief that the person is entitled to do so.

8. "Bodily Injury" sustained by an "insured" while "occupying" any covered "auto" while used in any professional racing or demolition contest or stunting activity, or while practicing for such contest or activity. This insurance also does not apply to any "bodily injury" sustained by an "insured" while the "auto" is being prepared for such a contest or activity.

D. Limit Of Insurance

Regardless of the number of covered "autos", "insureds", premiums paid, claims made or vehicles involved in the "accident", the most we will pay for "bodily injury" for each "insured" injured in any one "accident" is the Limit Of Insurance for Auto Medical Payments Coverage shown in the Declarations.

No one will be entitled to receive duplicate payments for the same elements of "loss" under this coverage and any Liability Coverage Form, Uninsured Motorists Coverage Endorsement or Underinsured Motorists Coverage Endorsement attached to this Coverage Part.

CA 99 03 07 97   Copyright, Insurance Services Office, Inc., 1996   Page 1 of 2

E. Changes In Conditions

The Conditions are changed for Auto Medical Payments Coverage as follows:

1. The Transfer Of Rights Of Recovery Against Others To Us Condition does not apply.
2. The reference in Other Insurance in the Business Auto and Garage Coverage Forms and Other Insurance – Primary And Excess Insurance Provisions in the Truckers and Motor Carrier Coverage Forms to "other collectible insurance" applies only to other collectible auto medical payments insurance.

F. Additional Definitions

As used in this endorsement:

1. "Family member" means a person related to you by blood, marriage or adoption who is a resident of your household, including a ward or foster child.
2. "Occupying" means in, upon, getting in, on, out or off.

156   BUSINESS AUTO

POLICY NUMBER: COMMERCIAL AUTO
CA 99 10 09 02

THIS ENDORSEMENT CHANGES THE POLICY. PLEASE READ IT CAREFULLY.

DRIVE OTHER CAR COVERAGE – BROADENED COVERAGE FOR NAMED INDIVIDUALS

This endorsement modifies insurance provided under the following:

BUSINESS AUTO COVERAGE FORM
BUSINESS AUTO PHYSICAL DAMAGE COVERAGE FORM
GARAGE COVERAGE FORM
MOTOR CARRIER COVERAGE FORM
TRUCKERS COVERAGE FORM

With respect to coverage provided by this endorsement, the provisions of the Coverage Form apply unless modified by the endorsement.

This endorsement changes the policy effective on the inception date of the policy unless another date is indicated below.

Endorsement Effective:	Countersigned By:
Named Insured:	(Authorized Representative)

SCHEDULE

Name Of Individual	Liability		Auto Medical Payments	
	Limit	Premium	Limit	Premium

Name Of Individual	Uninsured Motorists		Underinsured Motorists		Physical Damage	
					Comp.	Coll.
	Limit	Premium	Limit	Premium		

Note – When uninsured motorists is provided at limits higher than the basic limits required by a financial responsibility law, underinsured motorists is included, unless otherwise noted. If Underinsured Motorists Coverage is provided as a separate coverage, make appropriate entry in the Schedule above.

(If no entry appears above, information required to complete this endorsement will be shown in the Declarations as applicable to this endorsement.)

CA 99 10 09 02   © ISO Properties, Inc., 2002   Page 1 of 2

A. This endorsement changes only those coverages where a premium is shown in the Schedule.

B. **Changes In Liability Coverage**

1. Any "auto" you don't own, hire or borrow is a covered "auto" for Liability Coverage while being used by any individual named in the Schedule or by his or her spouse while a resident of the same household except:

    a. Any "auto" owned by that individual or by any member of his or her household.

    b. Any "auto" used by that individual or his or her spouse while working in a business of selling, servicing, repairing or parking "autos".

2. The following is added to **Who Is An Insured**:

    Any individual named in the Schedule and his or her spouse, while a resident of the same household, are "insureds" while using any covered "auto" described in Paragraph **B.1.** of this endorsement.

C. **Changes In Auto Medical Payments And Uninsured And Underinsured Motorists Coverages**

The following is added to **Who Is An Insured**:

Any individual named in the Schedule and his or her "family members" are "insured" while "occupying" or while a pedestrian when being struck by any "auto" you don't own except:

Any "auto" owned by that individual or by any "family member".

D. **Changes In Physical Damage Coverage**

Any private passenger type "auto" you don't own, hire or borrow is a covered "auto" while in the care, custody or control of any individual named in the Schedule or his or her spouse while a resident of the same household except:

1. Any "auto" owned by that individual or by any member of his or her household.

2. Any "auto" used by that individual or his or her spouse while working in a business of selling, servicing, repairing or parking "autos".

E. **Additional Definition**

As used in this endorsement:

"Family member" means a person related to the individual named in the Schedule by blood, marriage or adoption who is a resident of the individual's household, including a ward or foster child.

158   BUSINESS AUTO

POLICY NUMBER: COMMERCIAL AUTO
                                                                                                  CA 99 16 12 93

THIS ENDORSEMENT CHANGES THE POLICY. PLEASE READ IT CAREFULLY.

HIRED AUTOS SPECIFIED AS COVERED AUTOS YOU OWN

This endorsement modifies insurance provided under the following:

BUSINESS AUTO COVERAGE FORM
GARAGE COVERAGE FORM
MOTOR CARRIER COVERAGE FORM
TRUCKERS COVERAGE FORM
BUSINESS AUTO PHYSICAL DAMAGE COVERAGE FORM

With respect to coverage provided by this endorsement, the provisions of the Coverage Form apply unless modified by the endorsement.

This endorsement changes the policy effective on the inception date of the policy unless another date is indicated below.

Endorsement Effective	
Named Insured	Countersigned By

                                                                                             (Authorized Representative)

SCHEDULE

Description of Auto:

(If no entry appears above, information required to complete this endorsement will be shown in the Declarations as applicable to this endorsement.)

A. Any "auto" described in the Schedule will be considered a covered "auto" you own and not a covered "auto" you hire, borrow or lease under the coverage for which it is a covered "auto".

While any covered "auto" described in the Schedule is rented or leased to you and is being used by or for you, its owner or anyone else from whom you rent or lease it is an "insured" but only for that covered "auto".

B. **CHANGES IN LIABILITY COVERAGE**

The following is added to WHO IS AN INSURED:

CA 99 16 12 93   Copyright, Insurance Services Office, Inc., 1993

COMMERCIAL AUTO
CA 99 17 10 01

THIS ENDORSEMENT CHANGES THE POLICY. PLEASE READ IT CAREFULLY.

INDIVIDUAL NAMED INSURED

This endorsement modifies insurance provided under the following:

BUSINESS AUTO COVERAGE FORM
BUSINESS AUTO PHYSICAL DAMAGE COVERAGE FORM
GARAGE COVERAGE FORM
MOTOR CARRIER COVERAGE FORM
TRUCKERS COVERAGE FORM

With respect to coverage provided by this endorsement, the provisions of the Coverage Form apply unless modified by the endorsement.

If you are an individual, the policy is changed as follows:

A. Changes In Liability Coverage

1. The Fellow Employee Exclusion does not apply to "bodily injury" to your or any "family member's" fellow employees.

2. **Personal Auto Coverage**

    If any "auto" you own of the "private passenger type" is a covered "auto" under Liability Coverage:

    a. The following is added to **Who Is An Insured**:

      "Family members" are "insureds" for any covered "auto" you own of the "private passenger type" and any other "auto" described in Paragraph **2.b.** of this endorsement.

    b. Any "auto" you don't own is a covered "auto" while being used by you or by any "family member" except:

      (1) Any "auto" owned by any "family members".

      (2) Any "auto" furnished or available for your or any "family member's" regular use.

      (3) Any "auto" used by you or by any of your "family members" while working in a business of selling, servicing, repairing or parking "autos".

      (4) Any "auto" other than an "auto" of the "private passenger type" used by you or any of your "family members" while working in any other business or occupation.

    c. The Pollution Exclusion and, if forming a part of the policy, the Nuclear Energy Liability Exclusion (Broad Form), does not apply to any covered "auto" of the "private passenger type".

    d. The following exclusion is added and applies only to "private passenger type" covered "autos":

      This insurance does not apply to:

      "Bodily injury" or "property damage" for which an "insured" under the policy is also an "insured" under a nuclear energy liability policy or would be an "insured" but for its termination upon its exhaustion of its limit of liability. A nuclear energy liability policy is a policy issued by Nuclear Energy Liability Insurance Association, Mutual Atomic Energy Liability Underwriters or any of their successors. This exclusion does not apply to "autos" registered or principally garaged in New York.

B. Changes In Physical Damage
PERSONAL AUTO COVERAGE

If any "auto" you own of the "private passenger type" is a covered "auto" under Physical Damage Coverage, a "non-owned auto" will also be considered a covered "auto". However, the most we will pay for "loss" to a "non-owned auto" which is a "trailer" is $500.

C. Additional Definitions

As used in this endorsement:

1. "Family member" means a person related to you by blood, marriage or adoption who is a resident of your household, including a ward or foster child.

2. The words "you" and "your" include your spouse if a resident of the same household except for notice of cancellation.
3. When the phrase "private passenger type" appears in quotation marks it includes any covered "auto" you own of the pick-up or van type not used for business purposes, other than farming or ranching.
4. "Non-owned auto" means any "private passenger type" "auto", pick-up, van or "trailer" not owned by or furnished or available for the regular use of you or any "family member", while it is in the custody of or being operated by you or any "family member".

POLICY NUMBER:

COMMERCIAL AUTO
CA 01 21 02 99

THIS ENDORSEMENT CHANGES THE POLICY. PLEASE READ IT CAREFULLY.

LIMITED MEXICO COVERAGE

This endorsement modifies insurance provided under the following:

BUSINESS AUTO COVERAGE FORM
BUSINESS AUTO PHYSICAL DAMAGE COVERAGE FORM
GARAGE COVERAGE FORM
MOTOR CARRIER COVERAGE FORM
TRUCKERS COVERAGE FORM

With respect to coverage provided by this endorsement, the provisions of the Coverage Form apply unless modified by this endorsement.

WARNING

AUTO ACCIDENTS IN MEXICO ARE SUBJECT TO THE LAWS OF MEXICO ONLY – **NOT** THE LAWS OF THE UNITED STATES OF AMERICA. THE REPUBLIC OF MEXICO CONSIDERS ANY AUTO ACCIDENT A **CRIMINAL OFFENSE** AS WELL AS A CIVIL MATTER.

IN SOME CASES THE COVERAGE PROVIDED UNDER **THIS ENDORSEMENT MAY NOT BE RECOGNIZED BY THE MEXICAN AUTHORITIES** AND WE MAY NOT BE ALLOWED TO IMPLEMENT THIS COVERAGE AT ALL IN MEXICO. YOU SHOULD CONSIDER PURCHASING AUTO COVERAGE FROM A LICENSED MEXICAN INSURANCE COMPANY BEFORE DRIVING INTO MEXICO.

THIS ENDORSEMENT DOES **NOT** APPLY TO ACCIDENTS OR LOSSES WHICH OCCUR OUTSIDE OF 25 MILES FROM THE BOUNDARY OF THE UNITED STATES OF AMERICA.

SCHEDULE

Mexico Coverage	$ Premium

(If no entry appears above, information required to complete this endorsement will be shown in the Declarations as applicable to this endorsement.)

A. Coverage

1. Paragraph **7. Policy Period, Coverage Territory** of the **General Conditions** is amended by the addition of the following:

    The coverage territory is extended to include Mexico but only for:

    a. "Accidents" or "losses" occurring within 25 miles of the United States border; and

    b. Trips into Mexico of 10 days or less.

2. The **Other Insurance** Condition in the Business Auto, Business Auto Physical Damage and Garage Coverage Forms and the **Other Insurance – Primary And Excess Insurance Provisions** Condition in the Truckers and Motor Carrier Coverage Forms is replaced by the following:

    The insurance provided by this endorsement will be excess over any other collectible insurance.

B. Physical Damage Coverage is amended by the addition of the following:

If a "loss" to a covered "auto" occurs in Mexico, we will pay for such "loss" in the United States. If the covered "auto" must be repaired in Mexico in order to be driven, we will not pay more than the actual cash value of such "loss" at the nearest United States point where the repairs can be made.

C. Additional Exclusions

The following additional exclusions are added:

This insurance does not apply:

1. If the covered "auto" is not principally garaged and principally used in the United States.

2. To any "insured" who is not a resident of the United States.

CA 01 21 02 99   Copyright, Insurance Services Office, Inc., 1998   Page 1 of 1

162 BUSINESS AUTO

POLICY NUMBER: COMMERCIAL AUTO
CA 20 48 02 99

THIS ENDORSEMENT CHANGES THE POLICY. PLEASE READ IT CAREFULLY.

DESIGNATED INSURED

This endorsement modifies insurance provided under the following:

BUSINESS AUTO COVERAGE FORM
GARAGE COVERAGE FORM
MOTOR CARRIER COVERAGE FORM
TRUCKERS COVERAGE FORM

With respect to coverage provided by this endorsement, the provisions of the Coverage Form apply unless modified by this endorsement.

This endorsement identifies person(s) or organization(s) who are "insureds" under the Who Is An Insured Provision of the Coverage Form. This endorsement does not alter coverage provided in the Coverage Form.

This endorsement changes the policy effective on the inception date of the policy unless another date is indicated below.

Endorsement Effective:	Countersigned By:
Named Insured:	(Authorized Representative)

SCHEDULE

Name of Person(s) or Organization(s):

(If no entry appears above, information required to complete this endorsement will be shown in the Declarations as applicable to the endorsement.)

Each person or organization shown in the Schedule is an "insured" for Liability Coverage, but only to the extent that person or organization qualifies as an "insured" under the Who Is An Insured Provision contained in **Section II** of the Coverage Form.

CA 20 48 02 99   Copyright, Insurance Services Office, Inc., 1998

COMMERCIAL AUTO
CA 20 54 10 01

THIS ENDORSEMENT CHANGES THE POLICY. PLEASE READ IT CAREFULLY.

EMPLOYEE HIRED AUTOS

This endorsement modifies insurance provided under the following:

BUSINESS AUTO COVERAGE FORM
BUSINESS AUTO PHYSICAL DAMAGE
GARAGE COVERAGE FORM
MOTOR CARRIER COVERAGE FORM
TRUCKERS COVERAGE FORM

With respect to coverage provided by this endorsement, the provisions of the Coverage Form apply unless modified by the endorsement.

A. Changes In Liability Coverage

The following is added to the **Who Is An Insured** Provision:

An "employee" of yours is an "insured" while operating an "auto" hired or rented under a contract or agreement in that "employee's" name, with your permission, while performing duties related to the conduct of your business.

B. Changes In General Conditions

Paragraph **5.b.** of the **Other Insurance** Condition in the Business Auto, Business Auto Physical Damage and Garage Coverage Forms, Paragraph **5.d.** of the **Other Insurance – Primary And Excess Insurance Provisions** Condition in the Truckers Coverage Form and Paragraph **5.f.** of the **Other Insurance – Primary And Excess Insurance Provisions** in the Motor Carrier Coverage Form are replaced by the following:

For Hired Auto Physical Damage Coverage, the following are deemed to be covered "autos" you own:

1. Any covered "auto" you lease, hire, rent or borrow; and

2. Any covered "auto" hired or rented by your "employee" under a contract in that individual "employee's" name, with your permission, while performing duties related to the conduct of your business.

However, any "auto" that is leased, hired, rented or borrowed with a driver is not a covered "auto".

POLICY NUMBER:

COMMERCIAL AUTO
CA 20 71 10 01

THIS ENDORSEMENT CHANGES THE POLICY. PLEASE READ IT CAREFULLY.

AUTO LOAN/LEASE GAP COVERAGE

This endorsement modifies insurance provided under the following:

BUSINESS AUTO COVERAGE FORM
BUSINESS AUTO PHYSICAL DAMAGE COVERAGE FORM
GARAGE COVERAGE FORM
MOTOR CARRIER COVERAGE FORM
TRUCKERS COVERAGE FORM

With respect to coverage provided by this endorsement, the provisions of the Coverage Form apply unless modified by the endorsement.

This endorsement changes the policy effective on the inception date of the policy unless another date is indicated below.

Endorsement Effective:	Countersigned By:
Named Insured:	(Authorized Representative)

SCHEDULE

Vehicle No.	Description Of Loan/Lease "Auto(s)" Which Are Covered "Autos"	Other Than Collision Additional Premium	Collision Additional Premium
		$	$
		$	$
		$	$

(If no entry appears above, information required to complete this endorsement will be shown in the Declarations as applicable to this endorsement.)

The **Physical Damage Coverage** Section is amended by the addition of the following:

In the event of a total "loss" to a covered "auto" shown in the Schedule or Declarations for which a specific premium charge indicates that Auto Loan/Lease GAP Coverage applies, we will pay any unpaid amount due on the lease or loan for a covered "auto", less:

1. The amount paid under the Physical Damage Coverage Section of the policy; and
2. Any:
   a. Overdue lease/loan payments at the time of the "loss";
   b. Financial penalties imposed under a lease for excessive use, abnormal wear and tear or high mileage.
   c. Security deposits not returned by the lessor;
   d. Costs for extended warranties, Credit Life Insurance, Health, Accident or Disability Insurance purchased with the loan or lease; and
   e. Carry-over balances from previous loans or leases.

CA 20 71 10 01 © ISO Properties, Inc., 2000

COMMERCIAL AUTO
CA 00 51 12 04

THIS ENDORSEMENT CHANGES THE POLICY. PLEASE READ IT CAREFULLY.

CHANGES IN COVERAGE FORMS – MOBILE EQUIPMENT SUBJECT TO MOTOR VEHICLE INSURANCE LAWS

This endorsement modifies insurance provided under the following:

BUSINESS AUTO COVERAGE FORM
BUSINESS AUTO PHYSICAL DAMAGE COVERAGE FORM
MOTOR CARRIER COVERAGE FORM
TRUCKERS COVERAGE FORM

A. The **Operations** Exclusion under **Section II – Liability Coverage** of all coverage forms, except the Business Auto Physical Damage Coverage Form, is replaced by the following:

   9. **Operations**

      "Bodily injury", "property damage" or "covered pollution cost or expense" arising out of the operation of:

      a. Any equipment listed in Paragraphs **6.b.** and **6.c.** of the definition of "mobile equipment"; or

      b. Machinery or equipment that is on, attached to, or part of, a land vehicle that would qualify under the definition of "mobile equipment" if it were not subject to a compulsory or financial responsibility law where it is licensed or principally garaged.

B. The **Definitions** Section is amended as follows:

   1. The definition of "Auto" is replaced by the following:

      "Auto" means:

      a. Any land motor vehicle, "trailer" or semitrailer designed for travel on public roads; or

      b. Any other land vehicle that is subject to a compulsory or financial responsibility law or other motor vehicle insurance law where it is licensed or principally garaged.

      However, "auto" does not include "mobile equipment".

   2. The following is added to the definition of "Mobile equipment" in all coverage forms, except the Business Auto Physical Damage Coverage Form:

      However, "mobile equipment" does not include land vehicles that are subject to a compulsory or financial responsibility law or other motor vehicle insurance law where it is licensed or principally garaged. Land vehicles subject to a compulsory or financial responsibility law or other motor vehicle insurance law are considered "autos".

166   BUSINESS AUTO

POLICY NUMBER: COMMERCIAL AUTO
                                                            CA 20 15 12 04

THIS ENDORSEMENT CHANGES THE POLICY. PLEASE READ IT CAREFULLY.

MOBILE EQUIPMENT

This endorsement modifies insurance provided under the following:

BUSINESS AUTO COVERAGE FORM
BUSINESS AUTO PHYSICAL DAMAGE COVERAGE FORM
MOTOR CARRIER COVERAGE FORM
TRUCKERS COVERAGE FORM

With respect to coverage provided by this endorsement, the provisions of the Coverage Form apply unless modified by the endorsement.

This endorsement changes the policy effective on the inception date of the policy unless another date is indicated below.

Endorsement Effective:	Countersigned By:
Named Insured:	(Authorized Representative)

SCHEDULE

Coverages	Covered "Auto" Vehicle Numbers	Limit Of Insurance		Premium
Liability		$	Each "Accident"	$
Auto Medical Payments		$	Each Person	$
Personal Injury Protection or Equivalent No-Fault Coverage		Separately Stated in Each P.I.P. Endorsement		$
Uninsured Motorists		$	Each "Accident"	$
Underinsured Motorists (Indicate Only When Coverage Is Not Included in Uninsured Motorists Coverage)		$	Each "Accident"	$
Comprehensive		ACTUAL CASH VALUE OR COST OF REPAIR, WHICHEVER IS LESS, MINUS $ DED. FOR EACH COVERED AUTO, BUT NO DEDUCTIBLE APPLIES TO LOSS CAUSED BY FIRE OR LIGHTNING		$
Collision		ACTUAL CASH VALUE OR COST OF REPAIR, WHICHEVER IS LESS, MINUS $ DED. FOR EACH COVERED AUTO		$

CA 20 15 12 04   © ISO Properties, Inc., 2004

APPENDIX D - SPECIMEN FORMS 167

Specified Causes of Loss		ACTUAL CASH VALUE OR COST OF REPAIR, WHICHEVER IS LESS, MINUS $ DED. FOR EACH COVERED AUTO FOR LOSS CAUSED BY MISCHIEF OR VANDALISM	$

Vehicle No.	Description Of Vehicles That Are Covered "Autos"

Information required to complete this Schedule, if not shown above, will be shown in the Declarations.

A. This endorsement provides only those coverages where a premium is shown in the Schedule. Each of these coverages applies only to the vehicles shown as covered "autos".

B. The vehicles described in the Schedule will be considered covered "autos" and not "mobile equipment".

C. Liability Coverage does not apply to "bodily injury", "property damage" or "covered pollution cost or expense" resulting from the operation of any machinery or equipment that is on, attached to or part of any of these vehicles.

COMMON POLICY CONDITIONS

All Coverage Parts included in this policy are subject to the following conditions.

A. Cancellation

1. The first Named Insured shown in the Declarations may cancel this policy by mailing or delivering to us advance written notice of cancellation.

2. We may cancel this policy by mailing or delivering to the first Named Insured written notice of cancellation at least:

   a. 10 days before the effective date of cancellation if we cancel for nonpayment of premium; or

   b. 30 days before the effective date of cancellation if we cancel for any other reason.

3. We will mail or deliver our notice to the first Named Insured's last mailing address known to us.

4. Notice of cancellation will state the effective date of cancellation. The policy period will end on that date.

5. If this policy is cancelled, we will send the first Named Insured any premium refund due. If we cancel, the refund will be pro rata. If the first Named Insured cancels, the refund may be less than pro rata. The cancellation will be effective even if we have not made or offered a refund.

6. If notice is mailed, proof of mailing will be sufficient proof of notice.

B. Changes

This policy contains all the agreements between you and us concerning the insurance afforded. The first Named Insured shown in the Declarations is authorized to make changes in the terms of this policy with our consent. This policy's terms can be amended or waived only by endorsement issued by us and made a part of this policy.

C. Examination Of Your Books And Records

We may examine and audit your books and records as they relate to this policy at any time during the policy period and up to three years afterward.

D. Inspections And Surveys

1. We have the right to:

   a. Make inspections and surveys at any time;

   b. Give you reports on the conditions we find; and

   c. Recommend changes.

2. We are not obligated to make any inspections, surveys, reports or recommendations and any such actions we do undertake relate only to insurability and the premiums to be charged. We do not make safety inspections. We do not undertake to perform the duty of any person or organization to provide for the health or safety of workers or the public. And we do not warrant that conditions:

   a. Are safe or healthful; or

   b. Comply with laws, regulations, codes or standards.

3. Paragraphs 1. and 2. of this condition apply not only to us, but also to any rating, advisory, rate service or similar organization which makes insurance inspections, surveys, reports or recommendations.

4. Paragraph 2. of this condition does not apply to any inspections, surveys, reports or recommendations we may make relative to certification, under state or municipal statutes, ordinances or regulations, of boilers, pressure vessels or elevators.

E. Premiums

The first Named Insured shown in the Declarations:

1. Is responsible for the payment of all premiums; and

2. Will be the payee for any return premiums we pay.

F. Transfer Of Your Rights And Duties Under This Policy

Your rights and duties under this policy may not be transferred without our written consent except in the case of death of an individual named insured.

If you die, your rights and duties will be transferred to your legal representative but only while acting within the scope of duties as your legal representative. Until your legal representative is appointed, anyone having proper temporary custody of your property will have your rights and duties but only with respect to that property.

Index

A
Accident (defined), 55
Acquire (defined), 11
Additional insured- lessor
 Endorsement, 78, 87
Alternative dispute resolution
 Proceeding (ADR), 63
Appraisal condition, 43
Arbitration, 63
Assignment, 48, 53
Audio, visual, and
 data electronic equipment, 117
Audit condition, 49
Auto
 Acquired after policy inception, 11
 defined, 55
 equipment coverage, 32
 leased/hired with driver, 109
 leasing and rental concerns, 87

B
Bailee condition, 48
Bankruptcy condition, 47
Bodily injury (defined), 56
Borrowed auto (defined), 9

C
Cancellation condition, 52
Care, custody, or control
 Exclusion, 23
Causes of loss, physical damage, 32
Changes condition, 52
Checklist, commercial auto, 119
Clean-up costs, 57
Collision cause of loss, 32-33

Commercial auto checklist, 119
Commercial lines manual (CLM), 1
Completed operations exclusion, 26
Comprehensive cause of loss, 32
Concealment condition, 47
Conditions
 common, 51-53
 general, 47-51
 loss, 43-47
Consequential damage v.
 Direct damage, 31-32
Contingent coverage, 88
Contractual liability exclusion, 21
Conversion coverage, 89-91
Coverage extensions, 19-20
Coverage symbols, 5-9
Coverage territory
 Condition, 50-51
Covered auto designations, 5-14
Covered pollution cost
 or expense, 16, 27, 57
Customer's auto (defined), 115
Customers sound receiving
 Equipment coverage, 117

D
Damage to tires exclusion, 36
Declarations form, 2
Deductibles (physical damage), 39
Definitions, 51-59
Demolition contests exclusion, 36
Designated insured endorsement, 109
Diminution in Value, 39
Direct damage v. consequential
 Damage, 31-32

Domestic employees (defined), 22, 71
Drive away contractors Endorsement, 104
Drive other car coverage, 95-99
Driving schools endorsement, 104
Duplicate payments (med pay), 73-74
Duties in event of loss condition, 44
Duty to defend, 17

E

Electrical breakdown exclusion, 36
Electronic equipment exclusion, 37
Embezzlement, 89-91
Emergency vehicles endorsement, 103
Employee (defined), 58
Employee as insured endorsement, 83, 114
Employee as lessor endorsement, 116
Employers liability exclusion, 21-23
Endorsements, 101-118
  Additional insured – lessor, 78, 87
  Designated insured, 109
  Drive away contractors, 104
  Driving schools, 104
  Emergency vehicles, 103
  Employee as insured, 83, 114
  Employee as lessor, 116
  Explosives, 109
  Garagekeepers coverage, 84, 114
  Hired auto as owned auto, 79
  Individual named insured, 83, 98
  Injury to leased workers, 111
  Loss payable clause, 115, 118
  Mobile equipment as auto, 101, 105
  Mobile home contents Coverage, 105-107
  Multi-purpose equipment, 110
  One-way rental, 91

Pollution liability, 116
Professional services, 107
Public transportation autos, 111
Registration plates, 108
Rental reimbursement, 112
Repossessed autos, 107
Rolling stores, 110
Second level coverage, 93
Secretion coverage, 89-91
Snowmobile, 108
Sound receiving equipment, 103
Stated amount, 113
Tapes, records and discs coverage, 113
Underinsured motorists coverage, 118
Uninsured motorists coverage, 118
Wrong delivery, 110
Estimated premium, 49-50
Examination of books condition, 52
Exclusions
  liability, 20-28
  med pay, 70-73
  physical damage, 36-39
Expected or intended injury exclusion, 20
Expenses incurred (defined), 69
Explosives endorsement, 109

F

Family member
  as insured, 83, 98
  defined, 70, 74, 97
Fellow employee exclusion, 22
Final premium, 50
Forms, specimen, 133
Fraud, 47
Funeral service expenses, 67, 69

G

Garage operations (defined), 115
Garagekeepers coverage

Endorsements, 84, 115
Glass breakage coverage, 34

H
Handling of property exclusion, 24
Hired auto
  as owned auto endorsement, 79
  coverage, 78-81
  physical damage coverage, 49
  rating information, 81
  symbol, 8

I
Individual named insured
  endorsement, 83, 98
Injury to leased workers
  endorsement, 111
Insured
  defined, 58
  who is an, 18-19, 69
Insured contract (defined), 59-61
Inspections condition, 53
Insuring agreement
  liability, 15
  med pay, 67-69
  physical damage, 31

JKL
Labor costs coverage, 33-34
Leased worker (defined), 61
Leasing concerns, 87-94
Legal action against insurer
  Condition, 45
Liability
  coverage, 15-29
  exclusions, 20-28
  insuring agreement, 15
Liberalization condition, 48
Limit of insurance
  liability, 29
  med pay, 73
  physical damage, 39-41

Limited liability company (LLC), 10
Limits, required, table of
  (by state), 127
Loading and unloading
  (discussion), 24-25
Loss
  conditions, 43-47
  defined, 31, 61-62
Loss payable clause
  endorsement, 115, 118
Loss payment condition, 45-46

M
Mechanical breakdown exclusion, 36
Medical payments
  coverage, 67-69
  exclusions, 70-73
  insuring agreement, 67-69
Misrepresentation condition, 47
Mobile equipment
  as auto endorsement, 101-102, 105
  as covered auto, 12
  defined, 62
  exclusion, 25
Mobile homes contents
  Coverage endorsement, 105-107
Mopeds as autos, 5
Motorcycles as autos, 55
Motor homes as autos, 55
Movement of property exclusion, 25
Multi-purpose equipment
  Endorsement, 110

N
Named individuals coverage, 96-98
No benefit to bailee condition, 48
No-fault auto symbol, 7
Nonowned auto symbol, 9
Nonownership
  coverage, 77-85
  liability insurance, 81-83
  property damage coverage, 84

rating information, 84-85
Nuclear hazard exclusion, 36

O
Occupying (defined), 70, 75
One-way rental endorsement, 91-92
Operations exclusion, 25
Other insurance condition, 49

P
Pedestrian as insured, 69
Permanently installed (discussed), 38
Permissive use of auto
  (discussed), 10
Personal auto coverage, 98
Physical damage
  coverage, 31-41
  exclusions, 36-39
  insuring agreement, 31-34
Policy period condition, 50
Pollutants (defined), 63
Pollution exclusion, 26-28
Premium, estimated, 49

QR
Racing exclusion
  liability, 28
  physical damage, 36
Radar detection equipment, 37
Reasonable belief for auto
  use scenarios, 72-73
Reasonable expenses for med pay, 68
Registration plates endorsement, 108
Rental coverage concerns, 87-94
Rental reimbursement
  endorsement, 112
Repossessed autos endorsement, 107
Respondeat superior theory, 19
Rights of recovery transfer
  condition, 46
Rolling stores endorsement, 110

S
Second level coverage
  endorsement, 93
Secretion coverage
  endorsement, 89-91
Semitrailers as trailers, 65
Separation of insureds
  (discussed), 58-59
Severability (discussed), 58-59
Snowmobile endorsement, 108
Social service endorsement, 114
Sound receiving equipment
  endorsement, 103
Specifically described autos, 8
Specified causes of loss, 32
Spouse an insured, 96, 98
Stacking of limits, 29
Stated amount endorsement, 113
Stunting activity exclusion, 36
Subrogation condition, 46-47
Suit (defined), 63
Supplementary payments, 19-20
Surveys condition, 53

T
Tapes, records and discs
  endorsement, 113
Trailer (defined), 65
Trailers as covered autos, 12-13
Temporary workers (defined), 58-59
Temporary substitutes as
  covered autos, 12-13, 83
Temporary transportation
  expenses, 35
Towing coverage, 33-34
Transfer of rights and duties
  condition, 53
Transfer of rights of recovery
  condition, 46-47
Two or more coverage forms
  condition, 51

U

Underinsured motorists
  coverage endorsements, 118
  coverage symbols, 7-8
Uninsured motorists
  coverage endorsements, 118
  coverage symbols, 7-8

VW

Vehicle theft fraud, indicators of, 129
War exclusion, 28
Wear and tear exclusion, 36-37
Workers compensation
  exclusion, 21-23
Wrong delivery endorsement, 110